D1642920

*Together
in Time*

Together in Time

RUTH AND ED ROYCE

Published by
British Association for Adoption & Fostering
(BAAF)
Saffron House
6–10 Kirby Street
London EC1N 8TS
www.baaf.org.uk

Charity registration 275689

© Ruth and Ed Royce, 2008

British Library Cataloguing in Publication Data
A catalogue record for this book is available from
the British Library

ISBN 978 1 905664 39 9

Project management by Shaila Shah,
Director of Publications, BAAF
Photographs on cover posed by models, by istock Photography
Designed by Andrew Haig & Associates
Typeset by Fravashi Aga
Printed in Great Britain by Athenaeum Press
Trade distribution by Turnaround Publisher Services, Unit 3,
Olympia Trading Estate, Coburg Road, London N22 6TZ

BAAF is the leading UK-wide membership organisation for all
those concerned with adoption, fostering and child care issues.

The paper used for the text pages of this book is FSC certified.
FSC (The Forest Stewardship Council) is an international network
to promote responsible management of the world's forests.

FSC
Mixed Sources
Product group from well-managed
forests and other controlled sources
Cert no. SGS-COC-2482
www.fsc.org
© 1996 Forest Stewardship Council

Printed on chlorine-free paper.

For Joe and Jack

Acknowledgements
We would like to thank Joyce, who has been a huge support and a good friend to us and to the boys. We are grateful to Joy for teaching us how to stay together in time and for writing the foreword to this book.

About the authors
Ruth and Ed have been married for twenty-three years, are very keen on wine and music, and live in the Welsh Marches with their two sons Joe and Jack, and Monty the cat. Joe is now midway through his secondary school years and Jack is finishing off at primary school.

Contents

The Our Story series
This book is part of BAAF's Our Story series, which explores adoption experiences as told by adoptive parents.

Also available in this series: *An Adoption Diary* by Maria James, *Flying Solo* by Julia Wise, *In Black and White* by Nathalie Seymour, *Adoption Undone* by Karen Carr, and *The Family Business* by Robert Marsden.

The series editor
Hedi Argent is an independent family placement consultant, trainer and freelance writer. She is the author of *Find me a Family* (Souvenir Press, 1984), *Whatever Happened to Adam?* (BAAF, 1998), *Related by Adoption* (BAAF, 2004), *Ten Top Tips for Placing Children in Families* (BAAF, 2006) and *Josh and Jaz have Three Mums* (BAAF, 2007). She is the co-author of *Taking Extra Care* (BAAF, 1997, with Ailee Kerrane), and *Dealing with Disruption* (BAAF, 2006, with Jeffrey Coleman), and the editor of *Keeping the Doors Open* (BAAF, 1988), *See You Soon* (BAAF, 1995) *Staying Connected* (BAAF, 2002), and *Models of Adoption Support* (BAAF, 2003). She has also written five illustrated booklets in the children's series published by BAAF: *What Happens in Court?* (2003, with Mary Lane), *What is Contact?* (2004), *What is a Disability?* (2004), *Life Story Work* (2005, with Shaila Shah) and *Kinship Care* (BAAF, 2007).

Foreword

During the last ten years, there has been a lively debate about how to support adoptive families with children presenting attachment difficulties and disturbed behaviours, leading to significant changes in the post-adoption services available. This debate has been led from the front line by people living and working with traumatised children through organisations such as Adoption UK and BAAF. Adoptive parents have spoken out about their search for help and have recounted what works for their children and what they have found most helpful. Professionals have voiced the need for more information and resources, and agencies have invested in training to increase awareness of adoption-related issues of attachment, trauma and contact with the birth family. Academic study and research have explored which interventions are effective in developing a secure base and building positive attachments for traumatised children. Everyone involved with adoption shares a common concern: that of offering children who cannot live with their family of origin the best chance for health and growth in a new family context. But the journey has not been smooth and the debate has created strong splits among practitioners and theorists, presenting confusing choices for adoptive parents. This book is a welcome contribution to this debate. It is not a book of answers, but one of discovery.

Ed and Ruth's story, told with remarkable honesty and integrity, is an account of their journey from childlessness to celebrating as a family. Starting from a place of confusion and despair, they invite us to share the tale of their search to find the necessary skills and resources needed for the job of parenting two emotionally damaged children. Ed and Ruth believed that they had reached the end of the road. From a dual perspective, each with their own anxieties, expectations, and vulnerabilities, Ed and Ruth look back on their decision to adopt, to the fear that their family was falling apart, to their experience of music and art therapy and to their decision to adopt a second time. They record not only their different feelings about the same events, but also remember the first time they shared their feelings with each other.

The two boys they adopt also have different presenting difficulties, showing that what works for one is not necessarily relevant for another. One child had strategies to protect himself from making close emotional connections and the other protected himself from intellectual expectations. Both were difficult to parent and both have shown bravery in working to overcome their fear of trust in adults. Told with humour, the story that unfolds is one of determination and hope, and is essentially a love story.

There are common issues for all therapists working with children in adoptive families, such as:

- the therapist's role in the team of people supporting the family;
- the effect of trauma on the developing infant's brain and the resulting impact on all areas of the child's functioning and relationships;

- the essential elements in the development of primary attachments;
- understanding the importance of a child's history;
- the effect on parents and professionals alike of living or working with a traumatised child;
- issues of loss and bereavement for all concerned;
- regarding parents as part of the healing team and not as part of the problem;
- using what happens between the parent and child as the focus of therapy.

From the basis of these commonalities within different therapeutic disciplines came the development of a range of interventions over the timespan of this book, some of which had been developed in the US under the heading "attachment therapy". These became associated with other, problematic practices, and as a result there was a loss of trust particularly in those methods that involved holding the child. This lack of trust inspired therapists to find therapeutic models that were safe and took account of the common issues of adoption. Ed and Ruth experienced such occasional therapeutic holding with their first child, but not with their second. They make no judgment about the effectiveness but indicate the importance for parents to understand what is happening. Armed with this understanding, they were able to make decisions that changed their family and empowered them to feel confident as parents. Most important for them was being welcomed as full partners in the healing of their children.

This is the story of one family and does not attempt to consider the spectrum of support services available to adopters, but it is nevertheless a book that should give hope to a community of people ready to listen.

Joy Hasler, Clinical Director, Catchpoint
January 2008

1

Mother of all meetings

RUTH

Late one Sunday night, after another violent weekend, exhausted and disturbed, Ed phoned Helen and told her we were finished, we'd had enough. After two years we were at the end of the road.

The next day at 12.55pm, clutching Joe's tiny hand, we walked into the office of social services. As we made our way down the depressing corridors decorated with NALGO advertisements and tatty "please wash up your cup" notices, I thought of Joe's birth mother and father. They had probably attended meetings just like this. I wanted only to go home and forgot the whole nightmare.

Joe was entertained by a social worker armed with a colouring book and crayons. We were taken into an interview room. Helen sat with her line manager on one side of the coffee table; Ed and I sat opposite. They pacified and reassured us; they didn't confront us. Looking back, I suppose there was no other intelligent option.

But a line was definitely drawn at that meeting.

We knew we were in much the same position as Joe's birth family had been a few years earlier. They needed support because of disability, deprivation and disadvantage. We were asking for it because we were caring for an exceptionally needy child. Social workers, psychologists and psychiatrists spend years training to do weekly one-hour sessions with children like Joe. We did 18 out of 24 hours on weekdays and 24 out of 24 at weekends.

As we drove home from this mother of all meetings, Joe sat in the back, flicking through his *Thomas the Tank Engine* book, oblivious to the drama taking place in his life. We were silent. I feared the future. Ed was angry. We were on our own. As far as the local authority was concerned, we were his legal parents – it was our problem. Even if they did care, they didn't have the know-how or the resources to help. They would pay towards therapy if we found somebody suitable. It was over to us.

We returned home with Joe, clinging to the thought that if we found the right person we could resolve the problem. But we knew nothing about therapy. Where should we start? Again, I thought this is how Joe's birth mother must have felt every time social services called a meeting and another decision about her children was made. Try as she might, she just couldn't get it right.

After hours on the internet and several long telephone conversations with the Keys Attachment Centre, a few hundred miles away, I was near giving up. By this stage the dining room table was laden with piles of documents, leaflets, reports and books. Finally, it was the list of symptoms on the website of the Evergreen Attachment Center in Colorado that convinced me we were struggling with an attachment issue.

I remembered a year earlier when Helen had asked me, 'Do you think he has made an attachment to you?'

'Yes, of course,' I confidently assured her. But I was talking about myself rather than him. How do you know if a child has attached to you? It's not a question most parents have to ask themselves. It's natural for parents and children to bond; attachments are formed because infants learn to trust parents who consistently meet their daily needs: feeding, cleaning, playing, holding and, most importantly, giving them all those looks of love.

Not so when you adopt a child whose first attachments have gone dramatically wrong. I didn't know this of course; I wasn't trained in psychology. Looking back, I did feel there was something superficial about our relationship right from the beginning, but I had no other children so had nothing to compare it with. It just didn't feel quite right, but I loved him so much that the idea that attachment was a problem for him didn't seem a possibility.

A friend mentioned a woman in Bristol she'd heard of from another adoptive mother, whose daughter had had therapy for attachment problems. It was tough, confrontational and intrusive, but it worked. I thought therapy was about helping someone to understand themselves, I couldn't see why it had to be intrusive and tough. I decided to phone this therapist to find out more. It was about to be the most important phone call of my life.

Preparing myself for the phone call, I thought back to the beginning when we were first getting to know Joe, aged four. There were signs then, but I just hadn't recognised them. We were taking Joe for an outing from his foster home; it was part of the introduction plan. In my ignorance I hadn't realised car seats had become so high tech! It was quite an operation to strap him in and make sure the correct clips held the straps in place. Terrified I would crush his tiny chest, I messed around with it for ages, annoying Ed and, I suspect, Joe too.

Anyway, we set off with him peering out of the window and me thinking, 'What do we talk about with him? Should I put a tape on?' *Wheels on the Bus* was creeping into my mind when he started to talk endlessly about china plates; telling us all about the "greedients" that went into them, how they were made, and the factories they were made in. Surprised by the topic he had chosen and the extent of his knowledge, we were thrilled that he wanted to talk to us, albeit in words we couldn't always decipher, but enough so we could get the gist. We sensed it was important and meaningful to him. I listened in a bewildered haze, wondering if he would ever stop. His knowledge and curiosity about this unusual subject staggered me. He told us how porcelain must be mixed into the clay, that the right amount was very important, and it would then go to the factory with the big ovens and cook to make plates, bowls, jugs, mugs and so the list would go on. He repeated the whole sequence again, never waiting for our response, just talking at us over and over again.

No need for *Wheels on the Bus*, I thought. Just let him chatter on. Ed drove in silence, equally amazed, I suspect, at this little person's need to tell us all about porcelain and its exceptional properties. One of his previous foster carers had said she thought Joe was very bright and that his poor language skills masked his real intelligence and ability. However, professional assessments had indicated only an average intelligence.

At last a moment of silence. He sat quietly as we manoeuvred round the roundabout. I glanced over my shoulder at him. He didn't notice because he was looking down; he seemed to be completely self-absorbed, oblivious to any external stimuli. Then he suddenly asked us: 'Where have all my "before people" gone? Didn't they like me?'

There was a stunned silence until I could put together a collection of words. They made little sense to him and even less to me. Shouldn't we be having this type of chat at another time and place, so we can concentrate on the matter at hand, look each other in the eyes and have a real heart to heart? No, as I found out later, children like to talk in the car because they don't have to make eye contact and the seat acts as a barrier, giving them safe distance. I drew breath and began again.

'All your "before people" loved you very much, but they didn't look after you properly so another mummy and daddy were found for you,' I stammered out.

'They were very sad to lose you but they are pleased you have another family.' I was less confident now, feeling on shaky ground. Was this a reasonable way of putting it? Nobody had given us advice on this cropping up so soon.

Thankfully we arrived at the playground. We scrambled out of the car, taking less care with the car seat this time as I was in much need of fresh air. Joe ran to the slides and we trailed awkwardly behind. We struggled to keep up with him as he dashed from one piece of equipment to another. At first it was fun; increasingly it became irritating. Was he trying to lose us? Already?! I thought, this was supposed to happen when they were sixteen years old, not after sixteen days.

I felt saddened about his "before people" but at the same time knew that his and their loss was our gain. He thought nobody liked him and that was why they had all gone away, whereas we, the grown-ups, see it as him being taken away and rescued. This threw me. What a burden for a four-year-old to carry. He blamed himself. I knew we must put him right but now wasn't the time or place. He came over, took my hand, and asked me to give him a swing. This was encouraging.

Ed leant against the frame of the swing, watching while I did the pushing. He looked even less at ease than I felt. Was it the Sunday afternoon crowds or was it Joe's unpredictability? He was darting from one activity to another, talking about something and then midway losing interest and changing to something else, often running away from us and trying to tag on to another family. Thankfully for the moment he was settled on the swings.

'Higher, higher!' Joe shouted.

If I let the swing slow down he started shouting in an

excitable and very forceful voice. He seemed determined to get his own way. Or was it a reaction to never getting anything his way? I pushed him higher until I thought, 'No, this is wrong, it's unsafe'. As soon as I stopped pushing he blurted out: 'What does "properly" mean?'

I was immediately thrown again. How on earth could I explain? I wasn't sure myself what it meant to look after a child properly. Social workers have to study to know the answer. I didn't want to talk about the people who had abused and neglected him. I wanted to say, 'Just forget them, it's not important, they don't deserve a child like you,' but instead I said, 'Well, they didn't look after you in a very loving way, "properly" means in a loving way.' I surprised myself with this explanation and it appeared to satisfy him.

His attention went to the rocking frog on a spring. He leapt off the swing and raced over to it when it became free. Ed and I were regrouping, so to speak, making our way across to the frog on a spring, when Joe suddenly fell off it and badly gashed his leg. I raced over and picked him up, offering comfort as any person would. He immediately, although in great pain, pushed me away. We tried to help him but he would have none of it. He hopped over to the bench and hugged his leg up to his chest. He looked so alone and we felt so incompetent. During the journey home I sat in the back with him and he let me cuddle him but it somehow felt unnatural – controlled and on his terms – although the gash was real enough.

The next day at morning coffee I had to confide in a colleague I trusted – she was a Mum, a "proper" Mum. It was bothering me...no, *Joe* bothered me, or at least his reaction to me did. 'It's like he is on guard all the time, putting up a barrier with words by either constantly asking questions or telling us about some topic in minute detail and then repeating it over and over again. If he's not doing that, then he flits from one thing to another, he never settles to anything. And then yesterday, when he fell and hurt himself badly, he wouldn't be comforted. It's not natural, even a cat would take comfort! He's keen to talk about his past life, in a very matter of fact way that could be interpreted as mature, but it doesn't feel right for a four-year-old.'

My colleague was the first of many well-intentioned people who gave me the wrong advice. She, like all the others, forgot that his experience of adults, so far, was not as it should have been. He had learnt to trust no one. He relied only on one person, himself. 'He's adjusting and getting to know you,' she assured me. 'Give him time, you'll see a different boy in six months.'

2

Happy birthday!

ED

September 22nd was my birthday and most years I just ignored it, hoping it would go away. This year was going to be different. I am not one to analyse my feelings. I just get up in the morning and get on with it. I do know I was tired and pretty pissed off. It had all got too much and I needed a break. I promised myself a day walking, mainly to get away from work and the rest. I spent hours staring at local maps and decided to walk from home towards Ross, down the Golden Valley.

The lads at work had been winding me up about the boss always taking time off, which was true, but very little of the lost time was given over to pleasure. I was feeling guilty as I sent them off to another job and sat down to a second cup of tea before I went off. I remembered that Joe had been nice to me that morning. He was probably wondering if I was coming back. That question had crossed my mind too.

It was a nice day, reasonably sunny and no rain. All boded well. I stopped at the shop and bought a packet of Cheddars with a bonus of "25% free!" to nibble on the way. Last time I ate Cheddars by the packet was on my first scout camp. I had been terribly homesick but ten packets of fat-soaked cardboard had pulled me through! I must be comfort eating or reverting to childhood. I walked through the grounds of a big house complete with lakes and a temple. Is this a good thing, spending a day on my own thinking? I have always got on all right in life by keeping deep thoughts to a minimum and by always keeping busy – it's a strategy that's worked well so far. Whenever a problem crops up, I just make the best of it. It worked out alright when Ruth got sick. We are still here, aren't we?

*   *   *

How did we get to this point? I know, exactly. Ruth wanted kids. I was never that keen. I hate football and couldn't cope with sitting through ballet classes. I went through with the visits to the doctor and hospital, holding Ruth's hand, looking on the bright side. I went to the social services adoption training courses, looking interested and keeping an open mind but all the time finding reasons not to adopt. But one night I realised if I did not agree I would lose Ruth. Not necessarily this week, maybe not next year, but one way or another I would lose her. So in bed I decided, come the morning, I would make the best of the situation and push on with life.

*   *   *

After a bit the parkland disappeared and I walked across fields filled with sheep. I learned from listening to *The Archers* that if you find a lamb without a mother, all you have to do is wrap it in the skin of another dead lamb and its mother will accept it as her own. That adopted lamb doesn't spend the next ten years making its new mum's life hell for trying to give it a chance. As humans we are supposed to be more intelligent but Joe doesn't seem to see that. I heard Bob Geldof on the radio saying that, after their mother died, he told his kids: 'You have had a crap life up till now. Get over it and get on with it.' He said they did. I do not think it is that easy.

The phone rang. I hate mobile phones. Every time it rings you imagine all sorts of things. He has refused to go to school, wrecked the house or Ruth has packed her bags. Someone wants to know where to send an invoice. Half of me would leave the phone behind but the other half has to take it in case I am needed. You can never get away. I answered; it wasn't important.

I passed a group of cottages. A small boy was absorbed in a delicate bit of digging, probably tormenting some innocent worm. His mother sat in the sun on a rug; she smiled as I walked by. I bet she's not terrorised by her little darling. I bet she doesn't spend all her time trying to understand his behaviour and thinking of new ways to outwit him. Perhaps I should be spending my time making models of the Houses of Parliament out of matchsticks or train spotting with Joe. As the Americans say, "spending quality time together". But I am constantly battling to keep control. Stopping him from creating chaos and wrecking the house. It is such a waste of time. I feel as if he is dragging me into his world of anger and sadness, and I can feel myself resisting and at the same time feeling guilty that I am not doing enough dad-type things. Maybe he would not behave like this if I made more of an effort! I am forty years old and I do not appear to be able to control my life. I am being run ragged by a seven-year-old and I do not know what to do. I have this picture in my head of a capable, mumsy woman who understands these children and can help them to come to terms with their problems. She can cope with all they throw at her and never raises her voice or gets angry. I want so much to be like her. The only problem is I haven't got the faintest idea how. About this point I decided I was doing way too much thinking for my own good.

At the edge of a wood I sat down and took out my sandwiches. Not as exciting as you would have thought as five days a week I spend most of my lunch times eating identical paté sandwiches and looking out at various rural scenes. Still, I had my Cheddars (what was left of them). I sat there contemplating life; it was peaceful, perhaps too peaceful. I am not good at being on my own for too long.

Radio is my salvation. I had brought a mini radio in case I got bored. With it plugged into my ears and tuned into a phone-in I was off again along a disused railway. Nice and flat and dead straight, full steam ahead, no obstacles in front. A woman phoned in, a whingeing type, moaning on about I know not what, and the host, a sort of shock jock, was giving her a really bad time. He was getting very rude even for a shock jock. I was certainly shocked. He sounded so angry and bitter. She burst into tears. I don't know which one had the bigger problem. I thought I don't ever want to be as sad, bitter or angry as these two, whatever happens in the future. I have got to sort out this child, and survive the process. He is not going to force me into giving up. The railway ended at a locked gate covered in barbed wire; I hoped this was not some sort of sign. A few days later I found out the shock jock had been fired. That was not going to be me.

It was getting late. I was going to have to phone home fairly soon. I had a fantasy of walking further, finding a B and B, staying the night, and walking and walking and never going back. By the time I got to the next village, I thought, 'I have got to ring'. I was pretty tired and I wanted a cup of tea. I tried the phone. No signal! Ah, a phone box. Not working! Only thing for it, head for higher ground. After a good climb I got a signal, made contact. Everything sounded calm enough. So far, so good. Walked back down to the village. Maybe get a pint. Pub closed. Nothing else to do but wait. I saw our car coming down the road towards me. I always look to see Ruth's expression. Not too

11

good. As she swept round the corner I could see Joe scowling at me from the back seat. Not a good day then. Did he hate me because I had gone off and left him or because I had come back? Truth is he had no more idea than I had. I must not let it get to me. It's my birthday and I have had a good walk – put on a happy face, blind him with cheerfulness.

The journey back was strained. Joe's conversation consisted of what he did not have and we had not given him; what we had done and he did not like and what he wanted and we would not give. Back home Ruth had made me a nice birthday tea of all his favourite things. That makes me sound jealous. I do not feel jealous. I just want life to be more pleasant, not in constant turmoil. He wanted to light the candles; he wanted this done just so and that just like this. His temper deteriorated. Things flew, chairs crashed, he screamed, he spat. Let's get him into the bath; he always seemed to calm down in a warm bath. Ruth said she could cope. I picked up the furniture and rescued what was left of the tea but my appetite had gone. I sat there wondering how many birthdays I had left.

The noise rose to a crescendo of screaming and crying. I do not need this. Ruth called me, I ran upstairs. He was rolling on the soaking wet bathroom floor in the foetal position crying and making wailing noises. This was not sadness – this was pure unadulterated grief. He looked like a mother whose only child had died. He was inconsolable. If Ruth tried to hold him and comfort him, he pushed her away. She lay on the floor trying to get near him. I was not sure I could cope with this. (I am not good at massive outpourings of emotion. I always turn over when *Eastenders* comes on!) I felt superfluous, standing there like some sort of a voyeur watching the scene at a road accident. Maybe that's where my problem lies. If I was more "touchy feely", we would all bond and all this misery would disappear. Perhaps I am pushing him away. No, I am not doing guilt.

It's not my fault. On the brighter side, could this be what we have been waiting for? Maybe he has let all his sadness go, and in the morning he will wake up positive and keen to get on with his life. Unfortunately it's not as straightforward as that. Truth is we are still waiting for that damascene moment.

After about an hour Ruth got him into bed; he had just run out of energy. So had we. We went to sleep at eight-thirty.

My day away had been good. I had a more positive view of the situation. I don't think I understood Joe's problems any better but I think I had a clearer picture of our predicament. I had decided I was not going to do guilt. We had to get some advice and strategies so we could control our lives. There must be someone out there who knows. It was as if sitting on the edge of that wood scoffing Cheddars had allowed me to look out at more than just the view. I went to bed exhausted but not, I think, from the walking.

3

The call

RUTH

I talked to Joy, the therapist, on the phone for over an hour. I told her how, during the first two years, I had pretended to myself and not acknowledged Joe's behaviour. Other mothers enjoyed and shared their children's ups and downs. I glossed over everything, avoiding the truth because it was impossible to explain – it was so far removed from their experiences. They assured me night terrors were normal, not knowing that my child's nightmares were real, from daily doses of watching Dad hit Mum, not from watching something too scary on the television. My child's compulsion to eat excessively stemmed from his early years of hunger; it wasn't a phase some children go through and then outgrow.

Somehow Joy just seemed to tune into my ranting and sensed my desperation. Other professionals had not come near to it. They had looked at everything from Joe's point of view without enough regard for us, the people trying to parent him. Their perspective was usually influenced by their own experience of having only birth children, and by theories from books. They didn't consider how it feels to be an adoptive parent.

Not only did Joy encourage me to talk freely, she asked questions that helped me to explain and, surprisingly, she told me about her own son. Unbelievably, she had seven children – a mix of birth, adopted and permanently fostered children. She was not what I had expected. I liked her.

The more Joy talked to me the more my confidence grew. When I said he wouldn't do as I asked, she didn't question my parenting skills (one psychologist had suggested I speak louder); 'After all,' she said, 'the professionals spent a year assessing you, wrote a thirty page report about you, and then sought approval from the great and good of society, so who am I to question your ability as a parent?' Instead, she asked me about what interested Joe – did he enjoy doing puzzles? What was his speech like? Was he interested in opposites? She asked for examples of his defiant behaviour. She pinned me down.

When I told her about his aggressive outbursts, she talked about rage. It was rage rather than aggression, and had we noticed if he was worse at certain times? Yes, we had. When we were crossing the road back to our house last weekend, a car came over the brow of the hill, and because Joe kept refusing to hold my hand, it came uncomfortably close. Joe's face drained of all colour and he screamed and ran around and then charged at me. Hitting and scratching me, he shouted abuse more likely to be heard in one of Her Majesty's Prisons than in a cottage garden in deepest Herefordshire.

'I don't know what this means,' I said.

'Fear and control,' is all Joy said.

'What do you mean?'

'We will come back to that when I see you for the assessments. Can your husband come too? It's best if both of you are present. And yes, you will all need to be involved in the therapy if that's what Joe needs. I can't perform miracles, but I can take a look at him for you, and if I think I can help I will,' she said in her reassuring kind voice. 'From what you are telling me, he is exhibiting textbook attachment disorder symptoms. So in theory therapy should work, but there are no guarantees. All children are different,' she said, bringing me right back to reality again.

ED

Ruth phoned this therapist she had heard of in Bristol. Life was complicated enough as it was, and although things were bad, I could not see how going there was going to improve things.

She was a vicar's wife. I had visions of roses around the door, sort of a Dorothy L Sayers character. Ruth was out when she rang back so I answered the phone. I must have sounded pretty desperate. I told her how nothing was working, we had no control, and everything we did seemed to make it worse. Everybody we asked was sympathetic but had no concrete advice on how to deal with the day-to-day problems of living with Joe. I felt it was all our fault; we had no idea what we were doing. She brought me up short. 'It is not your fault. Did you feel like this before this child came into your life?' No. I knew that for a fact. I thought I was a reasonably strong, well-balanced person before I met Joe. Not the gibbering idiot I seemed to be now. Well, at least she was not blaming me for my failure to cope.

Over the recent months I had been to a number of meetings with local professionals who, in that annoyingly calm way they have, seemed to suggest that maybe *I* had the problem. I now realise, at that time, most of these people had very little idea about attachment, but could probably find a few things I was doing wrong. I once asked one of them what I should do when Joe was about to throw my fax machine through the window (it happened). 'Tell him you know how he feels,' was the reply. I can remember thinking, 'I'll get you to come round and fix the window!'

I told Joy all this and she said, 'How ridiculous! That's no good. Parenting these children is different. You have to think differently. When you ask him to do something and he refuses, do you "count to three or there will be a consequence"?'

'I do,' I said, 'but the trouble is that on one and two he ignores me, then he starts to move before three, so I go to three-and-a-half, and he moves a bit further, so I go to three-and-three-quarters.'

'If you do that he is in charge, he is making the running. Next time, say "I am going to count up to three in my head".'

I stopped dead. Yes, he would not know what number I was up to. It was like the clouds had lifted and the sun came through. Here was a person who, over the phone, had understood my feeling of total impotence and failure.

One of the hardest things for the adoptive father in this situation is the feeling of having absolutely no authority. For years I had run a business, employed people, supervised contracts, dealt with clients. I wasn't Richard Branson but I managed. I sorted out problems and controlled situations. Here I was, in my mid-forties, totally unable to control a child and my life.

You sometimes read an article in the newspaper about a captain of industry who rules with a rod of iron but at home his kids run rings around him. Well, I felt like that but a thousand times worse. I felt I had no way of making Joe do what I wanted. I had a good friend I could talk to but he did not really understand. When I told him what Joe did, he would say, 'Well, I would not stand for that from my son'. What he meant was that if his son did that he would give him a good clout around the ear. In fact, what would actually happen would be that he would threaten to clout his son and his son would back down and the problem would be solved. I could not do that. I would never hit Joe. I could not threaten to hit him. Any sort of penalty I thought up he would say, 'go on then'. Where did I go from there?

Joy had shown me a different way.

I couldn't wait till bedtime. I tried it. It worked. I remember the look on his face; for once he was not sure what was happening. I knew what was happening. I was in control. That one phone call had given me what the other experts had failed to do. A bit of usable advice I could understand. I am a practical bloke, I can build things, repair things, but I need to understand how they work to fix them. Otherwise, it's as if I am just sticking a screwdriver in until something goes bang. That was what I had been doing with Joe and it was only a matter of time until either he or we went bang. If Joy could help me to understand how he worked, I might be able to keep him running even if I couldn't fix him.

For me it was a turning point in my life. I realised that with the right help we could at least learn to manage his behaviour, and with luck, help him with his problems in the future. I could not wait to go to Bristol. For the first time in two years there seemed to be someone who understood and might rescue us.

4

The journey

ED

Following the phone call I felt we could make progress. Joy's idea had worked and I felt better about the situation. But the problem was that even if I could control a few aspects of our life, this was just a drop in the ocean. Now the desperation had subsided, I was beginning to realise how much we were going to have to do. Could we do it? Joy could obviously help us to cope but she was a "therapist". I was brought up to think that seeing a therapist was self-indulgent – it belonged to the world of the rich and famous with too much money. I had this nagging thought in the back of my head: Pull yourself together! You should be able to sort this out yourself. He's only a seven-year-old child, and aren't all therapists phoneys with funny accents?

I remember in *Steptoe and Son* (I am a big fan) an episode when Harold goes to see a psychiatrist after trying to strangle Albert while sleepwalking. The psychiatrist keeps asking Harold the size of his mum's Bristols! I hoped Joy was not going to ask me any embarrassing questions about my relationship with my mother.

As we drove over the Severn Bridge into unfamiliar

territory, I was beginning to think this was not such a good idea. Joy lived in this huge estate that looked like a war zone. This cannot be right. What happened to the roses around the door? Where were we going to leave the car? The wheels would be gone by the time we came out. We rang the doorbell. Joy appeared.

She was tall, looked like she knew what she was doing and she did not have a funny accent. I relaxed and wondered if the RAC carried spare sets of wheels! We went in, Joy spoke directly to Joe and we were ushered into what appeared to be the sitting room. We sat down. I was desperate for a cup of tea. I was waiting for the offer and a nice cosy chat. No luck. In all our visits to Joy I have never been offered a cup of tea. No time to mess about, it was straight to a big box of musical instruments in the corner.

I knew Joy's husband was a vicar but surely we were not going to have a couple of verses of "bringing in the sheaves". They certainly seemed like missionaries living where they did. But no, we could pick whatever instrument we wanted. I found a strange thing like a piece of stainless steel exhaust pipe with a spring on the end. It made a pleasant sound and I settled back to be creative. At first Joe couldn't make his mind up; there were too many to choose from. But then he saw a large drum at the back. He dragged it out and started hitting it like a man possessed. He had that look on his face. It said 'I am going to hit this so hard there will be nothing left'. He looked at Joy to make sure she knew what he was doing.

She seemed quite happy and off we went into free expression. Ruth and I were twanging and pinging and Jo was bringing the house down. I could not see how any of this was going to help anyone and certainly not the neighbours. Joy halted proceedings eventually and changed the rules. We would take it in turn to lead and the others would follow. Everyone got the idea except Joe; he sort of tried but there was always that "look". Suddenly the top of his drumstick came off; it rocketed through the air and bounced off the ceiling. We all collapsed in fits of laughter. I am no expert but this didn't seem very therapeutic. It was great fun but I could not see what good it would do. We calmed down. Joy said 'Well, Joe, I think you are very sad and angry. You do not want your mum and dad to help you and you are not happy to do as they ask.'

I was stunned that she had worked all that out from us making an unholy row. I asked how she knew. She said we could see how angry he was from the way he beat the drum and that he did not want to join in with "follow my leader". She had got it right without him knowing what she was doing. I started to look at the session in a different light. I saw how we interacted with the instruments as a family; how Joe behaved in different situations even while he was having fun. Time was up and we were ushered out of the door.

The wheels were still on the car. I asked Joe if he had had a good time. He said he had and next time he was going to play the cymbals. The drum had stood up to the pounding, the question was, would the cymbals? As we drove back across the bridge I could see the green trees of the Forest of Dean on the other side. I once heard a comedian describe it as the green fertile patch in the V between the Wye and the Severn. It felt like that as we neared home. I was glad to get back. It had been an interesting trip, and best of all, Joy had not asked me anything about my mum.

RUTH

Joe sat quietly in the back. We told him we were going to visit a lady who might be able to help us become a happier family and help him with his tantrums. He was surprisingly co-operative, no confrontation or opposition, apart from complaints about the length of the car journey. Perhaps he was relieved. He knew something wasn't right. From time to time he would talk about "narsty parsty". He told me he called him that because he was like a monster that wouldn't go away. Often his drawings showed "narsty parsty" in dark colours and always very large in comparison to other figures in the picture.

'He won't leave me alone. I tried putting him down the drain before school one morning but he kept coming up again,' he said in his sad little voice. 'And once I tried burying him in a grave where we collect the conkers, but he wouldn't stay there either.'

Maybe he was hoping the new lady would get rid of him. When he described "narsty parsty" I sensed his hopelessness. How could he get rid of this monster? I was unable to help him. This was beyond my understanding and left me frustrated and sad. For Joe it must have been terrifying.

As we drove across the Severn Bridge my mind was racing. I began to draw a mental picture of a music therapist. A lady in twinset and pearls playing Beethoven on the piano to lots of out of control adopted children. She would live in a large Victorian rectory with a beautifully landscaped drive lined with yews. Her vicar husband would work in his study at the front of the house and survey his parish.

I remembered Joy's voice. She spoke in an unaffected way, not a posh sort of accent, just standard. Yes, she would be a "no frills" person with feet on the ground. We desperately needed this lady. She was our lifeline, our last hope of keeping us all together. I was thoroughly exhausted and knew if Joe's behaviour didn't change soon I would cave in or snap. We drove in silence heading for what I thought would be the leafy outskirts of Bristol. The boarded up windows and razor wire on the roof of the public library were the first hints, but it was the shopping centre, or rather the collection of burnt out shops that really got us. 'This can't be right, she can't live in this place, it looks like a "no-go" area,' growled Ed.

We were tired and just wanted somewhere nice to go, where a kind lady would put everything right for us. This was horrible. We parked in front of her house. It had a pebbledash front, an overgrown garden and windows in need of paint, but it was considerably tidier than its neighbours. We were shocked by the general air of deprivation. One last glance to check the address before Joe enthusiastically rang the bell and the door swung open.

Joy immediately put her hand out to Joe, and said, 'You must be Joe, I am pleased to meet you'. Then she greeted us, but as soon as we were inside, she shook Joe's hand again and said, 'Congratulations Joe, you survived, you are a real hero'. He was baffled and so were we.

As we shuffled into the front room, a spaniel wobbled out from the kitchen. Joe used this as a chance to get away. He stroked it. I was distracted because something wasn't quite right about this animal. And then Joe blurted out: 'He's only got one eye'.

Joy laughed and explained his name was Bede, after the great scholar. I noticed she was dressed in simple trousers and blouse with open sandals. I think I was staring at her. She was as tall as Ed, or at least she looked that way to me. But I was so nervous I probably magnified her in my mind. I was on red alert whereas she was calm. She had a "no nonsense" firm way about her and at the same time she was kind and laughed loudly. Her style helped me to relax.

The house was a "no nonsense" place too, with an old sofa and chairs in the room where the assessment would take place; just an ordinary home. The most dominant features were the bookshelves that lined the walls up the stairs and in the hall. A piano, drums, cymbals and baskets of smaller instruments were in the assessment room. Joy sat on a chair whilst we took the sofa. Joe flitted around. He was hyper-anxious. Like us, he sensed this lady was different.

'Joe, can you sit down please? I want to explain to you why I congratulated you and why I think you are a hero.' He was intrigued. So he sat down.

'You know when you lived with your original family, your birth family, you found ways to survive. You looked after yourself. You were clever to do this, and a real hero because children shouldn't have to do that. It is the job of parents to look after children. They should keep their children safe. So you have done remarkably well to figure out a way of looking after yourself. But now you don't need to do this any more because you have new parents who will look after you and keep you safe.'

He listened for a while but then lost interest. She then spoke to Ed and me:

'It's important you understand what I'm doing so I will explain to you as we go along, and it's important for Joe to understand too.'

For the first time in two years I felt safe and included. Ed blurted out he could only play the trombone badly and I said it had been years since I played the piano. She laughed and said it made no difference, this wasn't about musical skills. Her frankness and confidence helped to put us at ease to choose our own instruments. I chose a shaker, Ed the wooden frog and Joe the bass drum.

'Interesting choice you've made, Joe,' said Joy. As he bashed away on his drum she explained to us: 'He chose that so he could dominate, take over and drown out any music you might make'.

She was right; the shaker and the frog didn't stand a chance. So then she suggested another game. All three of us were going to climb a big mountain together. Joe's job would be to choose the instruments we could take with us on our journey that might be useful. He loved this. He was in charge of us. I liked how Joy always referred to us as Mum, Dad and the Royce family.

Joy described the trees, birds and flowers as we

clambered up the slopes, all the time encouraging Joe to choose his instruments sensibly because mountains could be dangerous. Yes, there was snow on the peak, and she reminded him that we were on this journey too. We were there to help. He chose to take the bell because it might help to herd the goats, the large shaker for hitting any nasty animals and a drum to cook a stew. He draped them on his body as he climbed the mountain. Not once did he hand us an instrument. He struggled on by himself. He did glance at Ed occasionally but cut me out totally. He turned his back on me. This was hurtful but I was used to much worse.

When he reached the snow line Joy suggested we stop to set up camp. We would need wood for a fire, so he grabbed the wooden frog with its baton for kindling. He staggered about with bells, cymbals, and chimes dangling from his seven-year-old frame. The drum tied around his waist, a shaker under his arm, he struggled on to make a fire. We looked on as his frustration grew and yet he never once accepted Joy's encouragement to include us. Finally, she told him he must give us something to carry. It was too much for him. He selected a tiny bell for me; it was the size of a marble. He handed Ed one of the drumsticks, but no drum.

Eventually he collapsed in a heap on the floor as his frustration overwhelmed him. He flew into a rage, pushing and shouting at me. Then he retreated under the sofa. This was so typical of his behaviour at home: wanting to be in charge, never able to ask for help, and always hyper-vigilant for sounds, smells and sudden movements. When his anger left him he felt vulnerable and exposed, so he would hide in cupboards, under duvets or in the spare bedroom wardrobe for safety. It was like he was re-enacting past experiences.

Joy explained Joe's behaviour to us. Joe had learnt that control was essential for his survival. He found it impossible to share responsibility with us on his journey because we might let him down. That was his experience of adults so far. He had learnt that if he dominated and took control, then he would be safe. Giving us the least effective instruments was deliberate. He knew his drum would overpower us in size and noise. My little bell was forced to retreat into the background, weak and ineffective. Even when he included us, he gave us little scope to be effective or to have any control.

Joy tidied up the instruments and suggested Ed and Joe each choose a drum. She asked Ed to beat the drum and Joe to respond. Joe wouldn't wait to take his turn. He kept interrupting Ed, and he hit the drum so loud it made us feel uncomfortable. Doing something *with* his dad seemed impossible at the moment.

'Another strategy he has learnt,' said Joy, 'is to give the person closest to him the toughest time. So excluding you tells me you are the most significant people in his life. Take it as a compliment. His birth mother let him down, therefore he assumes, as you are closest to him now, that you will do the same. That is his experience so far and an intelligent and perfectly logical conclusion. Look on the bright side; at least he hasn't given up. His anger shows you are meaningful to him and he still wants to connect, unlike some children who appear to be well behaved but in reality have withdrawn. Their compliance is superficial, a shell for keeping others at a distance. He is definitely showing he hasn't given up and wants to get close.'

What an odd way to show you want love, I thought, but I could see some logic in it. With Joe you got what you saw. It probably sounds odd but there was a sincerity about him. He behaved as he felt; he didn't try to disguise himself. He wasn't behaving like this to manipulate us or to gain the upper hand. It was an illustration of how he felt inside.

Several times during the session, Joy asked Joe how he

was feeling; she never pushed him, just left it. However, as the hour was coming to an end she asked if he felt sad, mad, glad or scared. This was interesting. Joy explained to us that it was important for Joe to begin to recognise how he felt and to make connections between how he feels and how he behaves. It was early days, but asking if he felt sad, mad, glad or scared was a way of introducing him to his feelings. 'We will get a response eventually,' she said. 'In the meantime he has heard the words and, who knows, he might think about them. If you decide to go ahead you will need to reinforce at home what we do during therapy. If change is going to take place, it will be because of what you do at home every day, rather than what I do here for an hour a week. I'm here to guide you as much as him.'

What I immediately liked about Joy was her willingness to take risks. She used words that others dare not, describing Joe's behaviour in a way that I knew was right. She was the first to say "disturbed" and the first person who bothered to explain the meaning of "trauma" to me. And perhaps more importantly, how trauma affects children and how it can transfer to the people trying to take care of them. She cut through the jargon and just explained how it really was.

All this was said in front of Joe. There were no secrets here. I was surprised at first but soon realised how skilled she was in the way she did this. She included him in everything but at the same time used well-chosen moments to share crucial knowledge with us. She never raised our expectations too high and kept a reality check on how we were doing as a family.

Another surprise for me was Joe's willingness to believe in the narratives she created. His heart and soul went into climbing that mountain. He became totally engrossed very quickly in any imaginative setting she devised although he was poor at imaginative play himself. I don't mean he always co-operated, simply that he immersed himself in the roles Joy assigned to him, although he would often retreat under the sofa or become aggressive towards her.

Later Joy also explained about yet another of Joe's strategies. He had developed different heads to deal with the perceived threats and traumas in his early life, so that he could feel safe in different situations. Clever! So his behaviour reflected these heads he had created. At school he used his well-behaved head and at home we saw his angry head.

I read somewhere that separation from the mother in the first three years of a child's life causes the most damage. It is less damaging to older children. Joe was in and out of care or hospital from birth until he was permanently taken away from his birth family a few days after his third birthday. On some of the photos taken in his foster home when he had just turned three, he looks very confused, in shock even. His glazed, sad eyes are peeping out from a large pink fluffy blanket wrapped around him whilst he tries to eat his boiled egg and bread and butter soldiers.

When Joy talked about the different heads she used words like "dissociated behaviour". It was all very confusing and depressing. But it was important for us to understand his behaviour in terms of his heads rather than always viewing it as disobedient or naughty. It was equally important for Joe to understand this eventually. Ed was sceptical, I less so. It began to dawn on me how dreadful Joe's early life must have been. Neglect had left him unequipped to develop the most essential human skill of making relationships. Could Joy really change the way he viewed himself, the world and other people?

As we were leaving, Joy's husband emerged from his study. I noticed more books lining more walls. He introduced himself, shook hands, and gave Joe an extra friendly smile. We made small talk, mainly about Bede (the dog not the scholar), and departed before the next family arrived.

The Victorian rectory and yew-clad drive didn't matter now. We had made an ally. We drove back across the Severn Bridge, exhausted but hopeful.

5

Doubts and delays

RUTH

As the weeks passed by after the assessment, it felt as though we could speak of nothing else but the therapy. Should we or shouldn't we go ahead? If we did, and it failed, what then? If we didn't, we would probably fail anyway. After two years of relentless aggression and defiance, we were running out of energy. It was impossible for us to keep giving love when nothing but anger and rage came back. Joe's frantic controlling ways dominated our lives.

The autumn was a calmer time for Joe. Perhaps that's how life had been in his birth family. I knew the summer months had been wild times for them, with virtually no routine or comfort. But then we hit December and the scratching, hitting and hating us started again. This was the month he had been removed from his mother by social services, the month he spent so much time in hospital and the month of his birthday. We wondered why he had no photos of his first, second and third birthdays, then realised he had spent each of them in hospital. No major illnesses, just the day-to-day results of neglect: diarrhoea, burns and infections. The sort of neglect that doesn't hit the headlines or convince courts to convict, but the variety that gives root to muddled feelings, poor emotional and intellectual connections and delayed development.

One night I wanted to give Joe a bath. Ed hadn't returned from work. Joe was busy cleaning the taps and messing around with the water. I explained it was bath time and started to prepare the bath and undress him but he insisted on cleaning the tap. He got cross and then flew into a rage, throwing himself on the floor. The crying turned into deep sobs and he heaved his body on and off my lap as I knelt on the floor trying to offer comfort. This wasn't the usual tantrum, but something like it had happened before. He appeared to be helpless as he hurled himself around. I waited for him to calm down but he didn't. The tap seemed to have triggered a memory so disturbing that he couldn't disguise it. His only word throughout was 'why?' His grief lay exposed, as he lay naked on the bathroom floor.

Ed returned from work. Reacting to my desperation, he ran to fetch a book called *Helping Children Cope with Separation and Loss*, by Claudia Jewett, which we had read before Joe came to us. Ridiculously, we sat on the floor with Joe and frantically flicked through it hoping for an answer. After an hour, there was no change, and I felt he was in danger of hyperventilating, so I forcibly took him in my arms and placed him in the warm bath water. He protested, but the sensation of the water calmed him.

Social workers had warned us Joe might, like most children who had been in care, go through a period of mourning. It was generally considered better for their long-term health if they did, so Joe's grief reaction was no surprise to us, but the degree of his suffering was.

Joe talked a lot about his "before people", especially his two brothers who were now placed with another adoptive family. And although social workers and foster carers considered his relationship with them to be of little significance because he had constantly fought with them, even hurt them, we knew it was very significant. Possibly equal to his feelings for his parents. He gradually adjusted to having no "day-to-day brothers" as he called them, and accepted that he could still love them even if they lived elsewhere. Once he was putting a video of them into his special wooden box, when he said, 'They're in a coffin now'. When I asked, did he know what a coffin was used for, he replied 'it's for dead people'. He was six years old at the time, and it taught me never to underestimate children.

Joy found that Joe was able to talk about his past very easily. We thought this a good thing, but it seems that he intellectualised rather than allowing himself to feel about his family. 'It's another layer he has created to protect himself. The reality is too painful for him. He is bright, and realises that it pleases adults to hear him talk in this way; they feel privileged that he shares his memories with them, but he isn't really engaging with his past.'

I phoned Joy and told her about the bathroom incident. She reassured me because she agreed it was probably an expression of his grief, and although I didn't feel he was able to take much comfort from us, at least he shared it with us. We were able to be there for him.

Joe's grief was deeply affecting Ed and me. It was heartbreaking to watch a small boy struggle with so much personal pain. As he struggled, inevitably our own losses came to the fore. After all, we were childless, just as he was parentless. I had endured years of cancer treatment that saved my life, whilst Ed calmly carried on going to work and kept our lives cemented together. Now we were both trying to support Joe to come to terms with his loss.

* * *

Although I phoned Joy for advice, we still weren't sure about going ahead with therapy. It felt like such an enormous leap for all of us, and we were too caught up in the relentless day-to-day turmoil. We never knew how Joe would react; we were always on edge because he might attack us or break something. It started every morning with throwing his cereal on the floor, refusing to put his shoes on and then hitting me on the back of the head as I drove him to school. On one desperate occasion, I rammed the car into the hedge to stop him. He did stop, but not for long. I dreaded picking him up at the school gate. He would run off while other children happily held their mothers' hands.

Each day Joe would try to tell us how and where to sit, stand or even walk. He would change seating arrangements at the table, move placemats and cutlery. In the bathroom he would insist the toothpaste was placed just so. We would come in from the garden to find the living room completely rearranged or paintings in different rooms. This would inevitably end in a scene as we endeavoured to maintain some semblance of normality by putting our belongings where they should have been. It was like he wanted to control us by re-creating the chaos from his "before" life.

There were no boundaries for him. He deeply upset Ed and me when he broke our personal belongings. He targeted Ed's office, smashing art tools from his student days, and he broke my mother's pearl necklace, losing many of the tiny delicate beads and making it impossible to mend. Very little of the jewellery left to me by my mother has remained intact and Ed eventually had to put a lock on the office door.

One Saturday morning I was paying the milkman at the kitchen door. When I came into the dining room, Joe was there, his right hand full of soil taken from the conservatory. He hurled it at me. 'You left me alone, you went away, I hate you.' Fear of abandonment was another trigger for rage.

Later I learned that he should have helped me to clean up the mess, but at that stage I was still driven by trying to nurture and take care of him, rather than by common sense. Nobody had told me how to deal with fear of abandonment. Our four-day training for adoption didn't cover it; it is not a typical parenting skill. After an incident like this, Joe would deny all knowledge of it, like it had never happened. We felt more and more disconnected from him; if he was out of touch, so were we.

To the outside world Joe looked like an attractive, dark haired, blue eyed gorgeous little boy. He loved learning and was liked by his teachers – not as much by his peer group. He asked questions and was keen to lead in class activities. Often his concentration let him down and so he failed to succeed. His frustration would then be saved up and vented at home. Some of the teachers realised his behaviour was too controlling but generally they gave us the impression that sufficient TLC would put everything right for him. I was embarrassed when I tried to talk about attachment difficulties to anyone. It felt like an admission of the most fundamental failure.

Joe's controlling behaviour was beginning to irritate other seven-year-olds, in a way that hadn't bothered younger children. I sensed the children's disapproval and, to a lesser extent, that of their parents. Few party and tea invitations came his way. He was taking the path of his birth family; social exclusion, I think, is the official terminology for it. Ed and I found this increasingly stressful. It was difficult to have an unpopular child; it added to our own sense of isolation.

But life wasn't miserable all the time. Joe's innocence and honesty charmed us and made us laugh. After school one afternoon when he was eating his biscuits and drinking his milk he made a confession. I knew it was important by the way he delicately placed the biscuit back on the plate, paused, took breath and quietly declared that he held his "thingy" at school. My attention was immediate. Fearing the worst, I asked, what did he mean? 'I hold my thingy under the table when I am doing numeracy, it helps me think.' Soon after this, one of the mothers told me that Joe had proudly told her son that he knew the proper name for a "willie". According to Joe, it was called a "peanuts". Her son was very impressed.

Joe loved playing the "claw", a game invented by Ed. To be accurate, one Ed adapted from a movie he had seen a few years earlier. Ed would hold his hand like a claw behind a cushion or his back and chase Joe, making animal noises. This kept Joe entertained for many evenings up until the age of about eight. They would roll over the sofa and floor, Joe half believing the claw was about to get him. Sometimes I was summoned to help Joe, but mostly I looked on, while he enjoyed himself with his dad.

Another favourite was listening to stories. He always liked Ed to read to him but would be satisfied with audiotapes. If you wanted some peace, you could literally drug him with *Tintin* or *Just William* or in later years *Dad's Army* or Tony Hancock. The sound of voices comforted him and he loved new words. He constantly asked the meaning of words. We all enjoyed this part of our lives together, but we realised Joe's unmet needs from his earlier life were sapping us dry, and that his relationship with us wasn't going to change until he lost the need to be in control and felt safe enough to trust us to be his parents.

It wasn't until we were out cycling on Boxing Day that we finally made the decision to embark on therapy. Joe kept riding into the back of strangers, going off in the opposite direction and repeatedly threw his bike on the ground the moment something happened that he didn't like. We trailed behind him, keeping a safe distance and yet never letting him out of our sight, feeling useless and incompetent. We couldn't even manage a simple activity like cycling as a family. We had to admit to ourselves that Joe needed more than our love. His inner turmoil was way beyond our life experience and probably that of most people. So we booked our first therapy session with Joy for February. While we waited, Joe continued to throw volcanic tantrums many times a day.

One January afternoon he was in such a rage because he wasn't getting his own way that he fell against a plank of timber and cut his foot. He needed to be taken to hospital. He was unable to let us help him and hobbled to the bathroom, leaving a trail of blood and wrapped his foot in a towel, all the time holding back his tears.

Sitting in the back of our car trying to comfort him, I realised he was like a lodger in our house. He had lived with us for nearly three years now, but we were nothing more than house wardens to him. We might as well have been working in a children's home. The man in the fruit and vegetable shop meant as much to Joe as we did.

We felt very alone. We weren't able to share our worries with family or friends. The stress showed in our nightly need for wine. We had only ever drunk at weekends and usually when we went out. Now we were drinking every night. Therapy was looming; it was something other people did, not ordinary boring types like us. It was scary stuff.

But we were counting the days until Bristol.

ED

One of the reasons for the delay in starting the work with Joy was that social services insisted we were first seen by their own psychologist who was in charge of therapy for the county. The appointment was fixed for two o'clock one afternoon, and we headed for town. As we got closer the traffic ground to a halt. The river had flooded and the only road in was closed. Just what we needed. They already thought we were incompetent, now we were going to miss the appointment. We abandoned the car in a housing estate and started out on foot over an old railway bridge. We finally got to the meeting twenty minutes late feeling hot and stressed.

As I write this I find it hard to understand why I was so stressed. It was not my fault the river flooded. We could have just made another appointment. On that afternoon I felt my whole life was running out of time. If we did not get help very soon we were not going to make it. The psychologist and his team did not see it that way and after some general pleasantries informed us that, in the county's opinion, Joy was not a professional, more of a well-meaning amateur. They felt it would be better to have therapy within the county.

I asked, 'Who decides whether therapy comes from inside the county or out?'

'I do,' said the psychologist.

'Then who delivers the therapy in-county?'

'I do,' he said again. I asked the same sorts of questions I had asked Joy. The answers I received were vague and unhelpful. I said, 'In one phone call I got one hundred times more help, advice and understanding from Joy than I have got from you and you expect me to come to you for the therapy?'

'We could not see you for six months anyway,' he said.

I was getting more and more desperate. He asked Joe about his "real" mother. Joe didn't understand.

Ruth exploded. 'You have no idea what you are talking about! I am not staying here any longer.' She stormed out, I grabbed Joe, and ran down the corridor after her. Ruth does not often get mad but when she does you know it. When we got back to the car I said, 'That is it, we are going to Joy and we will pay for it ourselves. That way we're in control.' We drove home in silence.

*   *   *

In the past adoption was something you kept quiet about; there was a stigma attached to it. Possibly children were less damaged then, as they were usually given up at birth and so had more chance of bonding earlier with their adoptive parents.

When I told my brother, who lives abroad, that we were adopting a four-year-old boy, he said, 'Were his parents killed in a car crash?' I did not understand what he meant. 'Where have his parents gone?' he wanted to know. As a person from a somewhat sheltered background, he had no idea about why children are taken into care and probably didn't want to know.

Before we started the adoption process I had no more idea than he had. I can remember seeing a local family at the village fete. Mum had curly hair and so had four of the children. These were obviously her birth children and three others in tow were obviously not. I asked a friend about the family. 'They foster,' he said. I had only a vague idea of what fostering was. There was a huge woman in the town I grew up in. She fostered. I knew because she always pushed a pram, with what seemed at the time to be at least ten kids of all different shapes and sizes holding hands and strung out in a line behind. I always thought she looked happy enough. But why would this local family want more children when they already had four of their own? I could not understand. Since we adopted Joe we have become close friends with this family. They have adopted two children, and when things look pretty bad, we get together and share a sort of black humour you cannot share with others.

My parents were mystified when we told them what we were doing and as we started having difficulties they became increasingly distressed. They tried very hard not to criticise, but one day my mother let slip to Ruth: 'I do not know why you want children. It's not what it's cracked up to be, you know.' I said, 'Well that's easy to say for someone who's had two sons,' before Ruth had a chance to say anything.

They live miles away so we don't get to visit that often. This is a problem, as even during adoption assessment it is stressed that you need a solid family network to support you. We do not have one. This increases our sense of isolation. My parents were well into their seventies and could not have coped with Joe so it was probably a good thing they were 150 miles away. Every visit was stressful. He would race his toy car down the stairs, across the floor and crash it into the skirting board. I would say calmly, 'Joe, please do not do that,' trying to avoid a row.

My parents would say through gritted teeth, 'Don't worry, he won't do any harm.'

My mother would worry when he didn't eat his broad beans. She became upset and I asked why.

'You didn't tell me he doesn't like beans.'

'It doesn't matter, there are plenty of other more important things to worry about.'

Ruth comes from New Zealand; her father lives on the other side of the world and we only get to see him every other year. At first he resented Joe for, as he saw it, damaging our lives. He mistook Joe's confrontation for arrogance. Ruth felt he was envious of Joe's intelligence. I think he just felt sorry we were having problems. I get on well with him; he is another practical "Mr fix–it" type. I think he understood my feelings of inadequacy. He had married Ruth's mother, who was a widow, and inherited two stepchildren. I think he was unable to discipline them and had felt the same frustrations as myself.

Joe missed having lots of family around. Every Christmas and birthday he would moan, 'I haven't got many presents, is anyone else coming?' He comes from a big birth family, with lots of people hanging around, and I think he found it hard as fewer and fewer people came to visit and his invitations to tea dried up. People in the outside world did not realise what was going on. In a way we were lucky because Joe worried about his image outside the home. He rarely behaved badly at school and liked everyone to think he was good. He also got on well with babysitters and we managed to have the odd evening out. His concern about what people thought proved very handy.

One afternoon we were having tea in a café and he refused to behave. I warned him if he did not stop I would tell him off so that all the other customers would know what he was doing. 'You wouldn't dare,' he said, but I did. He was so embarrassed. He was more careful after that, and was usually pretty good when we travelled, which we did a lot.

Learning new skills was always hard. Joe could not understand that to improve you had to practice. Trying to ride a bike was a nightmare. Every time he fell off he would see it as failure, lose his temper, blame the bike, throw it down and walk off. He loved flying kites but if the wind dropped and the kite fell to earth, he would blame the kite and pull it to bits. This made things like learning to swim a long stressful process for all concerned. When he finally mastered something, he was often very good at it. But it seemed any achievement went against his belief that he was worthless. So many of the things we did with Joe were frustrating and hard work. It was like pushing a large rock uphill with someone hanging on to your coat tails.

* * *

I am clearly not a big fan of therapy; I do not have time for contemplating my navel but I knew we needed to get on with sorting things out, otherwise we were going to go under. Too many people we had seen up till then were full of "what ifs" and "maybes". What we desperately needed was a few "let's trys" and "hands on". It was no good intellectualising Joe's problems at this stage. The work needed to be very simple and straightforward. It also had to be fun. If it wasn't, we were never going to get him there, let alone get him to co-operate. If Joe thought he was doing us a favour, we would not see him for dust.

I knew it was going to be confrontational. Joe was

tough, he was not going to give up survival tactics that had served him well up until then, without a fight. Joy was obviously also tough and liked a challenge. She must have been, to live where she did. She was kind but I could see she believed in very strong discipline. It was definitely fun; I had had a laugh reliving my childhood on the maracas and I was sure Joe had enjoyed it too. All things considered, Joy was our best option. To be fair, she was our *only* option. I had great hopes that we could change his behaviour and that we could calm him down and make him easier to live with. But would we get to his deep-seated problems with drums and tambourines? I was not so sure. Were we putting a sticking plaster on a deep wound? If it stopped the blood flowing, I was all in favour.

6

The verdict

RUTH

From the outset Joy encouraged us to share our experience with other people. She recommended we select a few friends and she helped us make contact with an adoption support agency.

Sharing with friends was difficult for us because their experience of parenthood was, we thought, so removed from our own. Over the first two years we instinctively developed two stories. We told most of our friends absolutely nothing because we knew that to do so would be futile. Their children had given them very little grief, they were grown up, and the parents had moved beyond that part of their lives. We told a few other friends that there were problems, but gave limited explanations.

Looking back, I can see we were at fault. We underestimated some of our friends and probably would have got more support if we had asked. But we were quite a private couple, and although we had shared with friends when I was sick five years earlier, Joe somehow exposed our failings as adults. Cancer was not a failing, it warranted sympathy, whereas a naughty boy was generally deemed a nuisance, and we, as his parents, would be considered incompetent.

Someone said to me, I think she was a homeopath, that life changes like marriage, divorce, birth and adoption can also change friendships. We were certainly losing our secure world of friends that had, in a sense, become our family when I was sick.

*   *   *

Joy suggested we contact a worker named Rose at the West Midlands Post Adoption Service (WMPAS, now called Adoption Support). Rose advised us to let professionals know of our circumstances because children who have experienced trauma often have difficulty distinguishing between reality and fantasy. They confuse experiences from their past with the present. Traumatised children who have poor attachments often perceive their new parents as violent, cruel and rejecting, so they protect themselves by manipulating the truth. Joe might start making allegations against us.

We took Rose's advice and arranged appointments with our GP, the head teacher and social workers. We followed up each appointment with a letter confirming our conversation. This was a huge step for us. It felt like a betrayal of Joe but we knew Rose was right. There had been too many incidents where either Joe could have been hurt or he could have hurt one of us. This wasn't normal family life we were living and so we knew abnormal measures were needed.

Joy recommended books. I had already read a lot around adoption but very little specifically about attachment. One of the most helpful was the story of a girl called Katie who had enormous difficulties forming attachments. I could recognise many similarities between Katie and Joe. Even the picture of her on the front cover of the book reminded me of Joe. There was a photo of him taken during the first few months with us, when he was four years old, which showed the same sad washed out face, a sort of glazed expression of utter despair and faraway eyes that weren't connecting with the world. Not the look of a happy four-year-old. I began to realise there was no way we would ever have managed to deal with this alone.

As I learned more, I became angry at the ignorance of professionals who had simply not understood about attachment and how it affects us all. I know it isn't only adopted children who can have fragile or poor attachments. Other families have children with insecure attachments to one or both parents, but it became so obvious to me that children from the care system who have been severely neglected or abused are bound to have attachment difficulties, especially if the neglect or abuse happened in their early years. Expecting Ed and me to resolve Joe's cocktail of emotional needs, without therapeutic support, was bizarre. What were they thinking when they placed such a needy child with such an inexperienced couple?

About a year after Joe was placed with us we joined a local adoption support group. It proved to be an interesting experience for us but ultimately it changed nothing at home. I just wanted someone to give us practical advice. However, it did make me realise that Joe was, by far, not the worst case. Other children, it seems, exhibit even more troubled behaviour.

Even in this group, attachment wasn't mentioned in much detail. Certainly how our own attachment styles, as parents, impacted on the children wasn't considered. I owned up during one session to having some counselling because I felt Joe was digging up my past, but no one else wanted to go that way.

Joy was sure that Joe suffered from Reactive Attachment Disorder (RAD), due to severe neglect in those first three years of his life. She confirmed our fears. We appreciated her honesty but were deeply saddened too.

I found myself becoming angry with Joe's birth family. The world he originated from was a place where people were so dysfunctional they weren't able to perform the most fundamental tasks. They couldn't or didn't form a bond with their own children. Their children didn't trust them. As my resentment of his family grew stronger, my respect for Joe increased. Now I was beginning to understand why Joy called him a hero. He truly was an unbelievably brave boy. Joe was exposing me to a world I didn't especially want to visit. A place where people were cruel and lives were lived in complete chaos.

Trying to give Joe a balanced view of his birth family was a juggling act. When he talked about them, and in the early years he talked a lot about many members of his birth family, I found myself using phrases like, 'they just made mistakes' or 'they couldn't sort out all their muddled-up feelings' and 'they had mixed-up thinking'. I kept wishing there was a book that told you at what age, and how, to give your children particular pieces of delicate information.

As Joy explained her assessment to us, she also told us that we would need to parent him differently if we wanted to succeed. This became another hurdle for me. Up until now I had mothered Joe my own way. My natural instinct was to nurture, give him choices, let him explore the world at his own pace and think the best of him whatever he had done. However, what he needed was a mother who was authoritative, who restricted his life until such time as he felt safe enough to explore and make choices by himself. This was the beginning of my personal journey. Any hope of getting through to Joe needed a particular style of parenting called "tough love".

If Joe had been born to me, I would have sown the seeds of love and trust, so that we would be reaping the benefits of choice, exploration, learning, play and living as a family.

Instead, we were the recipients of poor planting, erratic pricking out and lack of appropriate nutrients. Our little seedling was having trouble taking root, staying upright and finding his place in the world. It all seemed upside down to me. If he lacked nurturing as a baby, then surely giving him loads of it now would be the obvious thing to do rather than getting tough.

As a baby Joe probably cried repeatedly and became full of rage because his parents didn't soothe him by touching, smiling, rocking, feeding, changing, making eye contact and reassuring noises. So, instead of learning to trust his parents to care for him and protect him, he would remain hungry, feel physical pain from having a cold bottle of milk shoved in his mouth, hear loud noises of shouting or music, have no eye contact and nothing to tell him that he was loved and important. More than likely he was totally ignored and just cried himself into an uncomfortable sleep. No doubt Mum did do some nurturing from time to time, but if the cycle of neglect occurred often enough to convince Joe that he was unsafe, then he would, quite sensibly, have developed his own protective layers.

To further protect himself, Joe had divided himself into different Joes with powerful different heads for different circumstances, so that he could feel in control. This behaviour, Joy explained, indicated the early stages of Dissociative Identity Disorder. Joe openly talked about his different heads and acted them out to the music. The loud drum was his angry head, which he used at home, the bells his clever head for school and the xylophone his sleepy head for ignoring people and doing his own thing.

Mixed in with this was the possibility of post-traumatic stress disorder. From time to time, usually when he was excessively stressed, he would develop obsessive habits like rapid blinking, picking his nails and making holes in his clothes. Although they were less dramatic and made less impact day-to-day than his different heads, it made life harder for him and it seemed to be so unfair.

Joy wrote a report for us describing Joe's condition. This was shocking to read but it enabled us to understand him and to grasp how much we had to do to help him and ourselves. When you see something written down it does somehow affect your perception of it.

This is how she described some of the behaviour she observed.

- He tries to be in control and opts out if he can't do something his way.
- He is hyper-vigilant and suspicious of new situations.
- He is unable to accept an instrument or help from his mum.
- In musical conversation Joe was aggressive towards Mum but did admit this in discussion after the music.
- He tells what he is going to do rather than asks.
- He is unable to ask for help.
- He is unable to take turns.
- He can talk about his sad feelings but then turns this to anger which he targets at Mum over minor difficulties.
- He makes little eye contact.

She recommended:

- Intensive therapy for Joe in the context of his family.
- Regular support for the family from someone who understands the effect of living with a child who has suffered early life traumas.
- A meeting of all those involved with Joe so that there is a common understanding and a plan agreed by everyone.

Rose, the worker from WMPAS, took us over. She organised getting all the key professionals together, minuted meetings and chased people up to follow through. She supported us, gave us the right information, was uncritical of us and did it all while having a giggle. She was like a breath of fresh air and we will always be indebted to her. The agency she worked for was independent of social services and we found this helpful because we could talk to her more openly. At the same time, Emma, a social worker from social services, was allocated as our new support worker because Helen had been promoted. Helen had been brilliant throughout the early stages of the adoption but her knowledge of attachment issues was minimal. Emma injected humour into our situation. She was less well informed than Rose and Joy but was making it her business to understand attachment. We both liked her immediately. Ed was especially pleased because she was not one of those "head in the clouds, yoghurt eating, floral skirt, middle class, all theory and no common sense" social workers, as he called them. Emma was organised and, like Rose and Joy, liked a giggle (a necessary attribute, it seemed to us).

At this point I was one of the many foot soldiers working part-time for a manager in education who was well regarded professionally and a very decent person. He must have been, to put up with all my time off and increasingly erratic work style. One afternoon after a meeting we were talking about children. I knew he had three and one was disabled. My stress must have shown because as he poured me another cup of tea he told me that I was the expert on Joe now. There were no professionals, not even Joy, who knew as much about Joe as I did.

This man had spent sixteen years talking to consultants about his daughter's cerebral palsy and he knew far more than they ever would. They had the medical degrees but he lived with the condition day-to-day. So he was the expert.

I was only beginning to realise the enormity of the task ahead.

7

Therapy

RUTH

Joy suggested an intensive programme. From February we would come to Bristol every Friday afternoon for a session, stay over in a hotel, return to her on the Saturday morning, go off into Bristol for a few hours and come back again late Saturday afternoon for the final session.

We were up for it because we needed to feel there was an end in sight. In July it would be three years since Joe was placed with us. We told ourselves June was our deadline. We needed to see some change. Even a slight improvement would be enough for us to continue, but we needed a hint of a response from him.

The uncertainty surrounding the length of time needed for the therapy, the ongoing loss of earnings and hotel bills added to our already high levels of stress. But it wasn't the disruption and financial strain, as much as feeling for the first time in our lives completely outside the conventions we knew. Basically we were ordinary people trying to live an ordinary life but the therapy took us into another sphere. A place most people didn't understand or approve of. 'Therapy for children, how ridiculous!' I can still hear people saying it now.

The Friday session was about getting us comfortable again by playing instruments together. Not too demanding on Joe but challenging his need to control by having to co-operate. Inevitably he would defend himself by squeezing under the sofa, playing the wrong instruments, and never ever keeping still.

Usually Joy would recap from the previous weekend, asking about any deals she had made with him. Did he keep to them? There were rules in her house too, and so she spent time on the Friday reminding him of them. He must always look into our eyes when talking to her or us; he must use names when talking to us, ask when he wanted something or didn't understand and always do as he was asked.

We would leave feeling quite relaxed. Joe slightly anxious but ready to return the next day because basically he had spent the last hour having fun with Joy and us. We were all keen to get to the Italian restaurant, Joe for his pizza and tiramisu, Ed and I for a glass of wine.

It was an odd experience. The other families in the restaurant were going about their daily business whereas we were a family with a child having therapy. To other diners Joe must have looked like any seven-year-old. The fear that he would throw an enormous tantrum was never far from our minds. We could never be at ease.

Saturday morning was tougher. Joy insisted that Joe promptly do as he was told. We might be taking turns playing an instrument, playing a role in a story, or simply making music together. This required him to co-operate, and co-operation requires trust, which he didn't have. He would defy Joy by trying to bite her, spitting at her and occasionally scratching her. I looked on in total amazement. Up until now no one else had been privileged to be the recipient of this behaviour. He reserved it for Ed occasionally and for me frequently.

Joy was quick to reassure us: for Joe to do this to

someone outside his family was a very good sign. Children suffering from attachment disorders will usually behave well for people outside the family because these peripheral relationships don't require intimacy and therefore don't pose a threat to them in the way family relationships do. So she must be getting through to him.

Sometimes the session would get stuck. He just wouldn't co-operate, would refuse to play instruments, follow instructions or just sit still for five seconds. He would defy Joy every way he could find. When this happened she would sometimes lay him on the sofa with his head on her lap and hold each of his hands in her hands. His legs would be up against the back of the sofa or sometimes she would ask Ed to hold his feet so he couldn't kick.

All the time she did this he would refuse to do whatever she asked. Sometimes it appeared to me to be a battle of wills. He definitely considered himself superior to Joy. I use the word "superior" because what I began to see was a boy who thought adults were idiots, and come what may, he was, at the tender age of seven, utterly convinced he knew best. Co-operation with an adult was threatening.

I found Joe being held distressing, especially the idea that I would eventually be doing it myself. Ed was less worried about it, and Joe was so aggressive that it did somehow feel right. If he didn't let me hold him, on my terms, then he would never truly experience being a boy and having a mother care for him. The time for intimacy between us would be lost if we didn't grasp it now. I would simply be someone looking after him or, in the words of Ed, 'an unpaid social worker cum prison warden'.

Joy explained that Joe needed to feel the physical security of being held. As a baby he had never experienced sufficient consistent care to convince him he was safe. His biting and spitting were all saying 'hold me, look after me, I feel lost and on my own'. I remember thinking, 'perhaps I would have been too soft if we had birth children'. At the same time, I resented having to be tough because I knew I wouldn't have done it that way if Joe had been born to me.

Joy advised us to keep Joe physically close to us as much as we could. 'Think of him as a toddler who needs reining in. He's not used to intimacy and closeness. You need to teach him. Touching is vital for him but touching on *your* terms. Sit him close to you on the sofa; don't let him sit on a separate chair. Always make him walk beside you and hold his hand. Although he may defy you now, as time goes on he will hear the message and gradually begin to obey. Being held is the beginning of feeling physically safe with you.'

Part of me felt it was unnatural to force Joe to sit on my knee, to make him give me a hug, and to touch him such a lot, until one day when I was talking to an elderly friend about how some families are tactile and physically affectionate whereas others aren't. She said her four children were all very tactile because she was, and children generally learn these habits from their parents. If the parents expect a hug whenever they leave or return, then that becomes the norm. So I decided making Joe touch wasn't such an intrusion after all. I would grab him if necessary and insist on a hug every time we parted, even when I was just going to the village shop. Words weren't enough.

Joy was right, I knew she was, and if it was unnatural, then adoption of older children who have been traumatised was also unnatural. Perhaps it would take something unnatural to re-tune Joe. He was like one of those huge wooden radios from World War Two that wouldn't quite tune into the station because the static interfered with the sound too much.

During one of these holding moments, Joy explained about the importance of facial movements and how babies attune to their parents. They do this all the time their parents play with them, look into their eyes and smile and stroke their hair – always with the same, consistent love.

Joy assured us that Joe wasn't too old to learn trust through touch. I was sceptical but trusted her. I had tried "round and round the garden" and all the usual tickling type games in the early days but it had usually resulted in a tantrum. I would be more assertive this time around. I would start by playing little games on his hands, then arms and finally face. I was sure he would find it silly and odd but he loved it. Was he actually craving for me to take charge and wrap him in my arms?

The music, or at least the sounds we produced, were often not especially pleasing to hear, but we kept on playing: Ed and I in rhythm, Joe doing his own thing. There was something irresistible about the beat of the drums. I couldn't stop myself from joining in even when Joe created chaos on the cymbals; the rhythm absorbed us and drew us in. Even though we each started out with our own beat, somehow we blended to become one. Interspersed with the beat were the magical sounds from all those odd little instruments Joy had in her baskets. Even when Joe deliberately went against the rhythm it was soothing and satisfying as we inexplicably stopped on the same beat. It was, I suppose, us adults controlling a situation in a fun way. Joe often added one last beat after the finish, but nevertheless he did get the message that we had decided when to end the music. During the time we saw Joy, the sounds Joe produced and the manner in which he produced them changed dramatically.

We would leave the Saturday morning session on an emotional high, heading for "Bristol Explore" or the Zoo. Joy encouraged us to have fun and enjoy ourselves as a family. Presumably this was to reinforce Joe's place in the world with us, and to show him that, even if the past hour had been hard for him, life could be good.

It never ceased to amaze me how Joe could be bouncing off the walls in Joy's house and then, half an hour later, like any child of his age, enjoy all the "hands-on" science exhibits at "Bristol Explore". What was even more amazing was the fact that he didn't mind going back to see her later in the afternoon before we drove home. I could only think that deep down he was searching for something that might take away the emptiness and loneliness for him. He knew Joy connected with him in a way that no other person had.

The last session was usually at about four o'clock and was, I think, intended to wind him down, to make sure we left on a positive note and sometimes for making "deals" to keep until the following week. In one of these sessions Joy filled up a bowl of water and asked Joe what colour water he would like. I think he chose blue. So colouring was added. She then placed plastic mugs into the bowl and began to tell a story about a family, using the mugs as the people. She poured water back and forth between the mummy and daddy mugs to illustrate the giving and receiving of love. More mugs were added for the children and love flowed between them all. Joe loved water play and immediately threw himself into this activity.

He poured love to and from adults and children with much vigour. Joy moved the story on to another level when she showed how Mummy and Daddy stopped giving and taking love; the water was gradually reduced to a tiny amount and eventually nothing remained in their mugs. In the meantime, the children were bobbing about in the bowl not getting any love and losing some of their own. Straight away, without hesitation, Joe said, 'That is me and my brothers!' I was astounded and very moved. As the children remained unloved they became scared and frightened. Joy asked Joe how they could protect themselves. He wasn't sure but suggested using the cling film, which was next to her. So Joy left some water in the children's mugs but wrapped them in layers of cling film. Joe was relieved and thought that was the end.

Joy then added two more mugs. These bobbed about next to the children. She said that if mummies and daddies don't give love to their children, social workers find another mummy and daddy to look after them because it is essential for children to be given love. As the story developed, Joy tried to pour water from the new mummy and daddy mugs into the children's, but because they were covered in cling film she couldn't get any love in and they couldn't give any out. What could they do? Joe pondered on this for a while and then suggested a pencil. 'Poke a hole in it Joy,' he urged, as though his life depended on it.

Gradually some love was poured from the forever mummy and daddy mugs into the children's mugs but the hole only allowed a few drops to get through. So they began to undo the cling film. Joe agreed this was the best thing to do and enthusiastically peeled it off. However, just as the child mug he was unpeeling was coming to the last layers, he stopped. He looked up at Joy and said, 'I think it's best to leave on the last bit of film, Joy'. She tried to persuade him otherwise but he was not having it. I think that layer is still on until this day. He can't quite let it go. His mistrust of adults is so deep.

One of the many books Joy recommended introduced me to the effect neglect has on an infant's brain development. The young child's brain is so soft and marshmallow-like, it is easily disturbed and damaged. However, because it is so pliable, it can be changed again. For children like Joe (and their adoptive parents), these discoveries give great hope. Research studies in the United States show very definite changes in the brain before and after attachment therapy. I found myself hanging on to any piece of knowledge that gave the slightest glimmer of light. This kept me fired up with enthusiasm, which we needed in container loads because, as predicted by Joy, Joe's behaviour at home and at school deteriorated. He would get worse before he got better. She was right; it did get much worse. There was no letting up.

At the time we didn't appreciate how much his moods

and behaviour affected us. We were so occupied with day-to-day living that we failed to see how tired and sad we had become. Joe's despair and sadness seeped their way into me, making me less capable as his mum. His extreme isolation and despair was unbearable at times, as was his all-consuming anxiety.

I also became aware that Joe was able to set me off into a rage. He found the buttons to push. Like most children, he instinctively worked out my emotional weaknesses, but unlike most children, he didn't have the skill to understand when to stop. There were no limits for him when he pushed my two weakest buttons, rejection and shyness. He knew I didn't like scenes in public, so he would deliberately choose a public place to endeavour to get his own way. Cafes were his favourites. It made some outings a nightmare.

The rejection button was even more powerful. It was the one that could send me off into space. I'm not talking about the day-to-day oppositional behaviour I have described earlier, I'm talking about the hurtful variety, like running away from me when all the other children happily hold their mums' hands, cuddling up to other women, breaking a special gift I had given him, but most of all just not wanting me to be his mum. The day-to-day opposition was very wearing and ground me down, but the rejection touched my past. Other failures and losses resurfaced. I thought my childlessness due to chemotherapy had been dealt with, "done and dusted" so to speak, but the more Joe rejected me the more I realised just how much I had lost. I would never be a mother in the true sense.

I recognised that Joe and I had much in common: he had lost his mother and was separated from his family; I had lost my fertility and was separated from my family. He was one of three siblings, the able-bodied squeezed between two disabled brothers. I was the youngest of three, in the shadows of my two much older needy siblings. We were both one of three, both the odd ones out.

Ed and I were becoming more aware of the importance of attachments past and present, and so did some soul searching, but generally we were in a state of emotional procrastination. We were too exhausted to be anything else. Looking back, I did a lot of hunting for cheap flights to New Zealand during this period. My instinct was to run away when life got tough, whereas Ed buried himself in his work. The office became his hideaway den.

Joy was very keen on the idea of looking after ourselves and strongly encouraged us to find time for each other: 'Be selfish if necessary, he will survive'. After all, he had survived much worse than us going away for a weekend. I don't think we managed a weekend but we did get a night away, and we did make the effort to get out more together. My state of mind improved because Joy offered us emotional support as well as practical help. Joe was floundering but at least he was still hooked, even if for the moment it was to Joy rather than to us; at least he was connected to another human being.

We would leave Joy early on Saturday evening, never quite sure what she had achieved but armed with new tactics to try out at home. Always before departing on a high note and full of enthusiasm, we would confirm our next appointment. Ed and I usually felt good about ourselves, and empowered to make a difference to Joe's life and our lives. Joe was usually exhausted but he never complained, and no matter how many times he had done battle with Joy, he always gave her a smile and a wave as we drove off.

ED

It was always a rush to finish work early, pick up Joe and get over to Joy's in time for the Friday afternoon session. Luckily it was usually a fairly relaxed meeting. We would play some music, discuss what we were going to do next morning and decide whether Joe had carried out the tasks he had agreed in the previous session. These tasks would be linked to reducing problems he acknowledged he had. If we felt he had tried hard, we would reward him on the Saturday. Joy called these agreements "deals"; some would call them bribery; I would call them incentives. Whatever you call them, they work. Right from the start Joe always wanted to know 'What's in it for me?' After percussion interaction loud enough to wake the dead, we would drive a couple of miles to an "out of town" shopping centre and check into a Holiday Lodge type of place – very popular with me on account of their low price for a family room. We would book in and Joe would sit on the bed and watch TV.

We had a Miniature Schnauzer who had to come with us. We could not afford kennels and she would have hated it anyway. I gave up asking if hotels would take a dog because they never did. I used to nip out to the car with a holdall, put the dog in and carry her past reception. She was always very well behaved and would curl up on the bed and go to sleep. She rarely barked and most of the time no one ever knew she was there.

One Friday I was sneaking the dog into the room and Joe had asked me to bring his doll. It was quite a sophisticated and life-like doll. It would talk to you and cry if you didn't feed it. Joe was very attached to it; it soothed him. Sometimes when children are neglected or have to take on parenting responsibilities at an early age, they miss out on some aspects of their childhood. Perhaps the doll allowed Joe to feel like a younger, more dependent child. On this occasion I had put the doll in the holdall with the dog and walked into reception. A couple was talking to the receptionist; all three turned to look at me as I came in. At that moment the dog moved, the bag moved, this set off the doll and the zipped up bag emitted a loud cry, not unlike that of a hungry baby! I kept on walking as if I had heard nothing. The three of them just stared as I walked through to our room.

There was a fake type of Italian restaurant on this site, filled with the contents of about ten junk shops. We always had frozen pizzas. Joe loved them, and we would have a bottle of wine. I can remember the wine tasted very good. After supper we would go back to the room and at about seven-thirty Joe would go to bed if we were lucky. This was usually when the reaction to the earlier session would set in. He would shout, jump on the bed and bang on the walls. I remember hoping the rooms on either side of us were vacant. Eventually we would manage to convince him it was about ten o'clock and not seven-thirty. We would all get ready for bed, turn off the lights and fall asleep before eight o'clock in the evening.

The Saturday morning sessions were always more confrontational. Joy would ask Joe to do a simple task such as to sit on my lap without moving for one minute. Time and time again he would fail and Joy would insist he start again. He would get more and more angry, he would try to hit, scratch and spit. She would hold him. He would calm down and after a while agree to do as he was asked. But he wouldn't manage it, and the whole process would start again. We realised this was proving to Joe that Joy was stronger than he was; that Joe wasn't in charge. Eventually, when he got the message that he was not leaving until he did what he was told, he would give in and carry out the task. Then we would play some music and have some fun.

The music seemed to cut through Joe's anger. We had to work together, and he was almost forced to join in with the rhythm. Joe forgot his rage and would let himself go. The physical exertion of bashing the drum or trying to change the shape of the cymbals got rid of his frustration and made him feel good. It helped on all levels. I remember thinking that Joe was like a computer using one type of operating system when everyone else was using another. As a result, no matter what we said to him, however many files we sent, he could not read any of them. For that short time, when we played music in a group, both operating systems worked together. We could understand each other. It was a sort of window that only opened when we played music. Trouble was, when the music stopped the link was broken. I hoped that if we got through to him for that short period, in the end he would realise it was better for him to work with us than against us.

At the end of the session we would walk out into the fresh air totally drained and exhausted. Sometimes we would just window shop. Joe had problems with shops. Most children want something they see in shops and nag you for it. Joe wanted everything in every shop. We figured if we showed him all the wares in all the shops he would get bored and stop. A sort of do-it-yourself cognitive therapy. When he was very young his birth mother apparently used to buy him what he wanted regardless of how much it cost or how much money she had.

The afternoon sessions were usually quieter affairs reinforcing the work done in the morning. Sometimes Joe would go through the same routines and refuse to sit still for one minute. On one occasion Joy asked us to leave with whispered instructions to wait with the mobile phone. I sensed Joy had done this before. We sat in the dark in the middle of this estate wondering how long it was going to take. We could be here for hours. What a way to spend a Saturday night. Fifteen minutes later the phone rang: 'Joe is ready now'. We picked him up and wearily made our way home. In the back of the car Joe seemed to relax. He was tired but I always felt he left at least a small amount of his anger with Joy.

While we were driving home, as Joe was looking at the backs of our heads, we asked him if he wanted to stop hurting people. He said he did. He had recognised he had a problem. We said 'Joy can help you'. I think he understood. Was it too much to hope that this was a step forward? When things are rough you tend to think in a negative way. It always seemed to me that if I said, for example, 'Oh, Joe hasn't hit anyone recently' you could guarantee he would do just that. I was scared to say anything in case it all went wrong. I can best describe it as two steps forward and one step back.

It felt like we were moving in the right direction, but although we were included, Joy was doing the work. We had to do what Joy was doing. I had to be the alpha male and it was going to be a struggle. I had always known that; what was different now was that I understood a lot more about what was going on. I now had an idea how to get there. The question was, was I strong enough to see it through?

8

Therapy in action at home

RUTH

Joy's matter-of-fact manner meant she broke through barriers, and cut to the core quickly. There was no pampering from Joy, just getting down to the work.

Nothing fazed her. Joe could verbally abuse and physically attack her but she would still talk and react in the same calm way, explaining why he was doing what he was doing. There was so much we learned from these sessions; in some respects they had as much impact on us as on Joe.

We applied our newly-acquired knowledge with vigour because we so desperately wanted our family to work. Some of Joy's advice was common sense but some of it felt like the reverse of what you might expect. For instance, to diffuse Joe's anger we had to do something unpredictable and creative. Like any child he needed routine, but he also needed irregularity to show him that we were ultimately in charge, and to introduce spontaneity into his life even if it meant doing crazy things. So there were times when we would start singing or dancing, or put pudding plates on our heads.

Some of the daily difficulties were made easier for us by simply reducing Joe's choices: putting out only two cereal packets instead of five, knowing that he hated one of them. He immediately chose the one he liked and didn't bother to complain that he didn't like the other. It came as a relief to him. We applied this method to all aspects of his life. It wasn't until years later that he sussed it out and began to question us about it; for a long time it helped us all to get through, reducing his and our own anxiety.

When he made his choice we always said, 'That was a good choice Joe, well done'. He gradually showed pleasure and a small smile would emerge on his slightly less troubled face. So, although it didn't always seem relevant at the time, years later we are reaping the benefits. Usually Joe makes the correct choice now although we do have to endure doubts and delays. He knows personal responsibility and making choices go together; whether he will be able to apply this knowledge throughout his life is another matter.

One tactic for gaining Joe's co-operation, like getting him to pack up his toys for example, would be to say, 'I'm counting to ten in my head and then something will happen'. He immediately obeyed. It empowered us, and although we never said what would happen, he never asked. If he deliberately left one toy on the floor, we had to find the time and energy to make him go back and complete the task. Sometimes I would stay close to him and even help him as a way of reaching a compromise.

This was often the case in the mornings. Up until then I was still dressing him for school. He was always difficult and he wouldn't co-operate so I decided to make a deal with him. He would put his socks on, I would put his pants on, he would put his vest on, and I would button up his shirt, and so on. We turned it into a game. Some mornings it worked, others it didn't but that was better than never working. It gave him choices as to what he would put on, gave me more opportunity to touch him, and developed trust by giving and taking.

Meal times were another battleground. It wasn't so much the food as eating it together. This made Joe's anxiety levels go through the roof; he found it too intimate and threatening, so our meals were sabotaged until we discovered the trick of eating earlier, before he got too hungry, and making it as much fun as we could. We were surprised how well these simple tactics worked.

With Joy's help I began to see that getting Joe to accept any rules or boundaries needed guidance that reduced his anxiety and would also change his view of us. He genuinely saw us as cruel when we asked him to put his train set away. Bizarre, really, but the images he had of people were distorted, and so he felt threatened by any form of discipline.

We endeavoured to stay calm no matter what Joe had done, but there were times when we showed our feelings by raising our voices because we are human and just couldn't help it. On a couple of occasions I smacked Joe on his legs to stop him from hurting himself or me – something I'm not proud of and it didn't do much for my self-esteem but it happened. Ed vowed never to hit Joe and never has, although Joe has committed some horrendous deeds designed deliberately to hurt Ed. We tried to structure discipline so that Joe would see some logical consequences for his behaviour. We usually waited for him to cool down before we took action. We always encouraged him to tell us his thoughts and feelings on the matter, showed as much empathy as we could, but ultimately explained to him that he was in this situation because it was his problem, not ours. We tried to be direct and firm and always ended in a way that connected us rather than distanced us from each other. So we would say to him, 'As a member of this family you need to obey the rules because all families have rules, otherwise everybody gets in a muddle and does and says things they shouldn't'. We hoped we were developing his skills to make choices and accept consequences in order to reduce his entrenched feelings of shame and failure.

Joe really couldn't cope with failure on any level. We began to understand that many of the episodes I called tantrums were actually his struggle to cope with feelings of worthlessness. Something as simple as the battery running out on his play mobile train could set him off; or the toothpaste missing his brush and landing in the basin. I began to see how taxing day-to-day life was for him: the level of anxiety he felt and his hopelessness every time something, in his eyes, failed or wasn't as he expected. Getting the balance right between empathy and discipline was hard for me. Ed was much more objective, clear and consistent. Joe could charm me and so reduce my efficiency in dealing with him.

One aspect of disciplining Joe, which had a disproportionate effect on him, was our tone of voice. There would only have to be a hint of loudness or sharpness and he would become excessively anxious and then aggressive. He often said my voice was too sharp and Ed's too loud. But it was his reaction that was distorted, not our voices. I knew from day one that he disliked loud or sudden noises, but it wasn't until working with Joy that I understood how much it affected his feelings and consequently his behaviour.

Another distortion, due to early neglect and scapegoating, was Joe's heightened sense of injustice. Any perceived unfairness or discrimination would be unbearable for him. The slightest suspicion that he was getting less, or was being treated differently from anyone, would rocket him into shouting abuse and attacking us. At school he would sometimes mistake harmless play for injustice and protect another child by fighting the supposed culprit when the child didn't need defending at all.

Joy taught us how to get Joe to own his behaviour, and not to let him think it was in any way our responsibility. We would take a cushion to represent his anger and say, 'Here, have your anger back. I don't want it, take it back, it belongs to you.' He looked baffled at first but his rage didn't escalate as it so often had. Words weren't always enough; doing something with a cushion was more powerful for him. Or if Joe was getting angry with me and shouting abuse I would say, 'I'm sorry you feel that way about me but I'm doing my best'. Again it diffused his anger – somehow it side-stepped him.

We worked at not letting Joe's rages affect us for very long. Ed found this more difficult than I did. No matter what Joe did, he was a child who needed forgiveness, and he never ever went to bed without a kiss, a cuddle and usually a story. Overdoing everything and stating the obvious all helped Joe to move on. So I spent a lot of time smiling, touching, hugging, rocking and playing with him, all the while telling him how much we loved him, how beautiful he was and that we were the luckiest people in the world to have him as a son. I exaggerated my words and expressions so that through his blurred and distorted image of the world he just might pick up my messages and make some sense of it all.

Ed was good at explaining everything to Joe. I worried that explaining his behaviour would somehow take away his innocence, but Joy reminded us that his innocence was taken away from the day his birth family let him down. Joe was more receptive to communication that was visual or had props of some sort. Ed spent hours in the sand pit building roads and towns with him. It was noticeable how difficult Joe found creative play, and he spent much of his time burying or breaking cars rather than building. He appeared to lack the internal stuffing required to be creative, and so instead he created chaos that reflected the chaos in his head. But he always loved stories being read to him and, in later years, developed a real flare for writing poetry.

We owned a small greenhouse, which I messed around in, growing bedding plants for the summer and the odd vegetable or two. I decided to involve Joe in this, hoping he might enjoy it. He loved it, especially watching the seedlings grow. Whilst we tended them, or in Joe's case drowned them, I used the opportunity to talk about growth, change and how the seedlings needed the right ingredients to flourish. And how it was our job to look after them. I have no idea if any of it went in, but I do know it was a restful time for him. Until he was thirteen, he grew something every year; last year he managed a crop of gourds.

Another activity he enjoyed was baking. Fortunately, we have a large kitchen so he could produce fairy cakes and flapjacks all day long if he wanted. The structure of a recipe and the satisfaction of producing something pleasant had a calming effect on him; there were so few spheres of Joe's life that were successful, and these activities were much more meaningful and important for him than for other children.

Joy also taught us to let Joe know from time to time how we were feeling. Again, we would have to make it obvious because he didn't have the skills to pick up the cues. So we would deliberately have conversations he could overhear like, 'I'm feeling really sad and fed up because Joe wouldn't eat his dinner. I worked so hard to make him a nice meal,' or 'I feel so mad with Joe. He has taken my hammer from the workshop again. How would he like it if I went to his bedroom and took his train set?' It seems really childish now, but at the time it made sense. It didn't make his behaviour worse and, who knows, maybe something got through to him.

Crying was another problem for Joe. He didn't cry often, but when he did it was an unstoppable eruption of tears and snot. This crying was equal in power to the rage inside him and mirrored his pain. So now I tried to encourage him to cry more frequently rather than build up to these occasional outbursts. If he fell over I would rush to him, hold him and comfort him and shower him with affection. It did work sometimes, but I got a few odd looks from other people; they probably thought 'she's treating him like a baby', which of course was exactly what I was trying to do. Sometimes, I would role-play crying to show Joe that it was OK to let go. He watched but I knew something inside him needed to change before crying could relieve his pain.

One day, when we were driving to school, Joe's head was down as usual and he had been preoccupied with his own thoughts when he quietly said to me, 'I'm like an Easter egg'. I asked him why he thought so (it was just after Easter) and he replied, 'because I'm all hollow inside'. This time I had to fight back the tears. It reminded me of how Joy described Joe's condition and how the therapy might help. She said, 'Think of Joe as a broken vase you have to repair by gluing it together. When you fill it up it holds water and you can put flowers in it but from time to time due to the early breakage it may leak, the cracks might let water escape. It will work but it will always be fragile.'

When you adopt children they don't tell you about the pain. Joe's was acute in those early years. Looking back I can now see that I was swallowed up by it. It is almost impossible not to be. Living with Joe's personal pain changed him and us forever. We are not the same couple because we have lived with someone whose torment and agony took us to dark places in ourselves.

Not all adopted children have Joe's degree of pain, not all children will be able to share it and not all adoptive parents will want or need to share it. We shared it not by design but more by default. We were expecting Joe to take a giant leap of faith to trust us to take care of him and help him to rebuild his life. But his early experiences had programmed him to protect his life rather than live it. We were asking him to replace his programme with new software, but he had no way of knowing whether it would work, or keep him safe. All we could do was to go on taking advice from Joy and hope that Joe would instinctively do the same.

ED

I think Ruth has a somewhat rosy view of the difficulties we encountered. She feels protective of Joe and finds it hard to describe the problems we had with him. She doesn't want to paint too negative a picture. I am probably more of a realist and I feel that if we do not say how it was, the reader will think we are just a couple of moaners making a fuss about nothing.

Before seeing Joy it was very hard work living with Joe. I would come home from work on a Friday night dreading the weekend. For Ruth it was worse, her weekend started at three-fifteen every Friday. We would often have two days of unrelenting confrontations from seven in the morning to seven at night. There would be battles over getting dressed, turning off the television, eating breakfast, going outside, not going outside and all before nine-thirty in the morning.

If Joe was not allowed to do what he wanted at the beginning of the day, he would feel he had to punish us for the rest of it, and a cycle of tit-for-tat would set in. He would go up to the bathroom to clean his teeth. Silence. Always slightly worrying. I would go upstairs to see what he was doing. More often than not he had spread various shower gels, shampoos, soaps and cleaning products all over the floor. If I sent him to his room while I cleared up the mess, he would become even angrier because I had spoiled his fun. Silence again.

After a spell in his room he would go downstairs to the kitchen and start to do some cooking. Probably baking cakes. We encouraged this as it was constructive and he was good at it. The problem was, in his angry state he would make mistakes, lose his temper and throw away large amounts of eggs and flour. We would be constantly blamed for making a noise and putting him off or for failing to buy enough, or simply the wrong, ingredients. Butter would be smeared everywhere, flour was tipped on the floor, and another area of chaos created.

Joe would manipulate any activity to make a drama out of it, and create problems so that he could blame someone else. This would fuel his anger and, in his mind, justify his behaviour. We were in a vicious circle of bad behaviour, confrontation, punishment and bad behaviour. Whole weekends would pass with us calming him down whilst clearing up one mess after another. The one advantage was that Joe used up so much energy during the day that by seven o'clock he was worn out and went to sleep. Trouble was, we were so drained that we followed him up to bed.

We went through a period when Joe cut the plugs from phone chargers and headphones. Luckily he realised the danger of mains voltage so he was not at risk. That accolade went to Ruth. One evening Ruth, in a fit of desperation at not being able to persuade Joe to switch off the computer, cut the mains cable with a bread knife literally in a flash. (Do not try this at home!) Once, on a particularly stressful family outing, while I was moaning to Ruth about the number of dents in the car, I reversed into a B and Q car park at high speed, failed to stop and hit a tree. I am usually a good safe driver, but there are times when you get so wound up it becomes impossible to concentrate and you just lose it.

One evening we had confined Joe to his room. He came out and said, 'Right, I am going to get you. You have had it now!' He stormed downstairs to the kitchen. We could hear him opening the knife drawer and rifle through. We were in our bedroom. I looked at Ruth. 'He is getting a knife,' I said. I looked around for something to defend ourselves. I grabbed the duvet to throw over the knife. We could hear him coming up the stairs. He stood in the doorway. 'You've had it now,' he said again, and from behind his back he produced a very nasty-looking carrot. We could not stop laughing, I think as much from relief as anything else. Ever since then I have found carrots slightly threatening.

After meeting Joy, life with Joe was still very hard. We understood that we had to use sanctions as a way of confining and controlling Joe. Sending him to his room seemed the best option. At least we could limit the damage to one place. The first night he would not do as he was asked I said, 'You have two choices: go to your room or I will take you myself'. He refused, so I held his arm and guided him upstairs.

'I'll just come out,' he said.

'I will just put you back in.'

'Then I'll wait till you go downstairs.'

I had a chair and newspaper waiting. 'I can sit here for as long as it takes.' Joe tried to leave the room. I put him back. He threw his toys at me; I ducked and reminded him he was breaking his own toys. He kept slamming the door till it broke; I took it off its hinges.

The stand-off at the bedroom door went on for about two hours. He started to panic that he was losing control of the situation. He started screaming and throwing things. I was beginning to think I might have gone too far. Ruth was waiting downstairs listening to all the shouting and crashing around. She could not bear any more. She came up the stairs crying and pleading for me to stop. I turned her around and sent her downstairs. I knew we had to do this. I felt I had to go through with it whatever happened. Joe slowly calmed down, and crawled into bed exhausted and sobbing. Ruth came up to comfort him and he went to sleep. This scenario played itself out over and over again for the next few nights, but the intensity reduced each time. We had gone to the wire.

From then on if we said, 'Go to your room', he went and he stayed there. Being able to physically control Joe was a last resort; we knew we weren't hurting him, but we worried that others might see it differently. If Joe said something at school, would we have someone knocking on our door? In practice, after the initial week of showdowns at the bedroom door, we rarely needed to help him upstairs. We only had to ask if he needed help and he would go.

One morning, a few years later, we could not get him to school. I was late for work, getting more and more annoyed, but Joe would not come out of his room to get in the car. I tried the 'Do you need help getting in the car?' routine. He called my bluff. I had to go through with it. By then he was big and pretty strong. I held his arm and he yelled, pulled away and ran down the stairs, arms flailing, screaming all the way. He ran through the house, and with arms outstretched, crashed through the glass of an open door. He cut his wrist, not badly, but there was plenty of blood. It shook both of us.

That morning I decided he was too big to hold safely. If I did it again one of us was going to get really hurt. That night I told him that my ability to hold him had kept him safe in the past, but I could not do it any longer. I tried to explain that in future I would not be able to stop him physically and he would have to take responsibility to stop confrontations from escalating. I think he understood, and since then we have always been able to sort out problems before total meltdown. Joe has learnt how far he can go before the situation becomes impossible.

Into his teen years now, we get 'You can't make me!' What can you say? 'No, I cannot make you. But fairly soon you will want to be taken somewhere or need some money for something and you may find me in an ungenerous mood.' Like most teenagers, Joe likes money and possessions, so after some protestations and pouting he does as he is asked. Perhaps like me, deep down, he is a realist too.

Joy showed us ways of breaking the cycle of confrontations. She explained how Joe was mixing up his anger with sadness: when he felt sad it came out as anger. And the angrier he became, the more adrenalin he produced, and the more this covered his sadness. He was becoming addicted to adrenalin. We were making things worse by losing our tempers, shouting, punishing him and generally failing to keep him safe. I can get a bit passionate. I tend to raise my voice when I get excited or enthusiastic. To Joe, with his heightened sense of sound, it was as if I was shouting at him. I had to be more careful and to stay calm. It was not easy.

We learned to defuse situations. One mealtime he became angry and smashed a plate on the floor. I said, 'Oh Joe, that looks fun,' and took another plate and threw it on the floor. He looked so shocked. I could see he was thinking: 'Are these people mad? This isn't right. If I throw plates on the floor they should get angry. I had better stop doing it.' These tactics don't always work, but you have to change your mindset. You have to tell yourself, 'It's only a couple of plates; I can buy some more tomorrow'. It sounds easy but it isn't. You have to adjust your values and consider what really matters in life. Doing the opposite to what is expected often works. Humour is great for defusing a situation.

One evening Joe tried to hit me and I went straight out to the workshop, returned with big boots, hard hat, goggles, waterproofs and thick gloves on. I looked pretty strange standing in the kitchen. 'Right, I've got my protective gear on, so I'm ready for you.' We all laughed, including Joe. He had his "are they mad" look on his face again. If you can think of one, a joke told at the right moment does wonders. The hard part is, just when you're at the lowest point clutching at straws, trying to keep your life together, how do you think of a joke?

We learned not to hold a grudge. As soon as we had a problem with Joe, or with each other, we would deal with it, make up, and as soon as possible try to talk about it. If he had to go to his room, we would bring him down fairly quickly and start again. It was very hard for me to forgive and forget and to put a smile on my face. I saw it as giving in. Ruth found it easier and would encourage me to make new starts. The longer Joe's resentment festered, the longer he had to plan his revenge.

We realised he had a deep-seated ethos of "payback" which he had probably picked up in his birth family. Joe believed that just as we talked about the consequences of his actions if we had to discipline him, so the consequences of our actions should lead to payback time. At first it used to be physical, but Joy helped us to convince him that it was wrong to hurt people, so he would target possessions instead. It was interesting that he assumed we had the same values as he had. One day I found one of my old videos with the tape unravelled and hanging out. I asked him about it and he said the damage was payback for something I had done previously. Joe valued videos more than most things in life, so saw this as the ultimate punishment, but to me it was just an old video I hadn't watched for years. Joe used to boast to us that, like the elephant, he would never forget. Often we would find our possessions damaged and when asked, he would say, 'I did it because two weeks ago you wouldn't let me use the computer'.

We have found that if we have to enforce a consequence, it helps to frame it in a way that makes it an automatic result of his actions and is not meant personally. Saying 'I am sorry you have to do without television tonight' distances us from the penalty. If we do not put it like this, Joe will just think that we're being nasty to him and will feel we're fair game for further retaliation.

Perhaps to parents of birth children all this strategy and intrigue read like a political thriller set during the cold war.

It was hard to keep up with all of Joy's advice; we had to think on our feet and be ready to change tactics at any moment. This was all the more difficult because Joe is reasonably bright, and as soon as you explained why he had to go to bed at eight, he would come back with a plausible reason why he should stay up till four o'clock in the morning to watch a horror movie.

Joy did much, but she couldn't answer all our questions or solve all our problems. I wanted someone to say, 'Here is a handout. Do exercises 1 to 50 and all will come right.' It was never going to happen. Every child in every situation is different and every adoptive family has to go on a different journey.

We have been lucky. I know that sounds strange after all I've said, but because Joe kicked off from the start, we were in no doubt he had problems, and to survive we would have to deal with them one way or another. We were lucky that we found Joy and that she was easy to work with. But sometimes it felt like trying to carry out gene therapy with only an encyclopaedia and some back copies of the *Lancet* to tell you what to do.

9

Whitsun half-term

RUTH

For the first time in nearly three years, and four months after beginning therapy, I stood back and thought, 'It is quieter and certainly calmer'. Ed arrived home on the Thursday night from work and enquired in his usual nonchalant manner as to whether "all was quiet on the western front". I remember thinking it was the sunshine and lightness of spring that were helping me survive this half-term but then I told Ed that it was Joe. It took me by surprise and Ed too. He didn't believe it at first.

As the half-term week had progressed, Joe had become less oppositional, even on the odd occasion doing as he was told the first time he was asked. He was more engrossed in playing with his toys and hadn't thrown any mega tantrums. He was less anxious, less intense and didn't irritate me so much.

Putting Joe to bed that night was more enjoyable than usual because he let me tuck him in and he was quite playful; but it was when I gave him his goodnight kiss that he really took my breath away. I kissed him and gave him one last hug, and as I pulled my head away he looked straight into my eyes, put his arms around my neck and pulled me towards him. He didn't kiss me, but for the first time he reached out to me, the first bit of real giving; up until that moment it had only been taking.

Slightly flustered I got up from the bed and as I stood by the door to take a last glance at him, he caught my eye. It's hard to describe that fleeting moment, but he had never before really managed a subtle interaction – very few interactions at all for that matter. He was so busy being on guard that he never had the energy or space to notice other people's feelings. I smiled at him and he smiled back. It was the first time I felt like his mum.

This half-term holiday was a major turning point for us all. We relished it but were apprehensive that his aggression would return as soon as he went back to school. It didn't. Throughout June he remained calmer and less "full-on".

I can't say he was an angel. He was still challenging and overpowering. Our lives were still dominated by his behaviour but somehow the rage had diminished. We now wondered, how long would it last? Joy assured us it would be unlikely that he would ever entirely go back to his former self, but he would regress from time to time, and yes, it was early days yet. By the end of term in July, we agreed that a rest from therapy would be good for us all. So we enjoyed the summer. We took a holiday in Italy and although there were tricky moments and the heat made Joe moody, it was by far the best break we had had with him so far.

Earlier in the year Joe had joined Cubs. He was eight years old and we decided he needed more social skills. He was lukewarm about it but as soon as he caught sight of the uniform he was keen. He liked the discipline and rituals, and took the raising and lowering of the flag very seriously. At the end of July the pack had a barbeque. We were dreading it because social events were so stressful. He would wind up the other children, always touch things (often breaking them) and generally get on everyone's nerves. He could never just blend in.

As we stood in the field watching the boys play football I noticed Joe edging his way over to them. Was he going to run off with the ball as he so often did? No he was standing next to the boy in goal and looked like he was trying to talk to him. Then to our amazement he was helping the boy in goal. Five minutes later he was on the pitch kicking the ball with the rest of them. He wasn't being disruptive; he was just fitting in.

When the food was dished out, Joe sat with the others, quietly listening and making the odd comment. He looked like one of them and he wasn't pestering us. As I got him ready for bed that night, he let me undress him and didn't fight his tiredness. He let me take charge and look after him. I loved it and he fell asleep within seconds.

About this time I noticed another change in him. From the first day he came to us, he suffered from nightmares and night sweats. He would go to sleep relatively easily but never sink into a deep restful sleep. The slightest noise, movement or smell woke him up. In this light sleep his body twitched like a poorly co-ordinated marionette and his head would be drenched in perspiration. Now he was sleeping deeper and didn't sweat. If lifted his arm up while he slept, it flopped down limp on the duvet. He didn't stir from his peaceful sleep.

Joe also began giggling and laughing like a little boy. Part of him had always liked to play tricks and have fun, but this new laughter was different. It was as though a fresh, spontaneous and real part of him was coming to the surface. When a friend from school pushed him on the makeshift swing Ed had made from old tyres in the garden, I stopped washing up, listened, and thought 'that is the first time I have ever heard him really giggle with another child'.

Over the summer months, for the first time in three years with us, Joe developed colds. He was always blowing his nose and even needed a few days in bed because he felt so unwell. This was unheard of for him; he was such a robust, fit and healthy boy. It seemed that as he let his emotional guard down and began to interact with the world, he also made himself susceptible to germs.

It was during the return to school in the autumn that we saw the most dramatic difference. His new teacher had been briefed about Joe's quirky ways: bright but inclined to take control, winding up his peers, easily distracted and unable to focus for very long. Week three of the term and Mrs Andrews called me aside when I was collecting him and my heart sank, fearing the worst. Whom had he upset now? Mrs Andrews considered the parents' evening in November too late to update me and wanted to tell me how different Joe was compared to last term. He no longer tried to dominate or felt he had to be in charge all the time. He was taking his turn and working better in groups. His concentration was much improved. He was able to get on without adult supervision and was producing some really good work. She was thrilled and considered his behaviour to be no worse than that of many others in his class. I bounced through the school gates clutching his hand and gave him the biggest smackaroo, as we called them in those days. He laughed and hugged me back.

So we passed our deadline. The therapy was working. What would we have done if it hadn't? If he had remained stuck, locked in? I don't like to think about it.

ED

When things are bad you know it. You never have any peace. Confrontations take up all your time. You can't concentrate and every time you start a project a crisis erupts and you have to stop what you are doing to sort it out. Unfinished jobs pile up around your ears.

As our world became calmer we began to relax. In the beginning, at work, I used to dread my phone ringing at about three o'clock in the afternoon. More often than not it would be Ruth in a state. 'You have got to come home now. I can't cope, I can't control him!' I'd try to calm her; we'd probably have a row; she'd put the phone down. I would have to throw the tools in the truck, pick up my two lads and rush the twenty or so miles home, dreading the devastation I would find. As soon as I walked into the kitchen Ruth would start to show me the teeth marks and the damage to the house. Yet another fun-filled evening lay ahead.

After Whitsun, the year we started to work with Joy, the phone did not ring in the afternoon. We could clear up and go home at the end of the day's work. I could walk through the kitchen door and see Joe drawing quietly at the table and Ruth cooking the dinner. 'What sort of a day have you had?' I would ask. 'Fine.' For most people this is normality, for us it was something very new. As Joe's anger subsided, he seemed to have more room in his life for friends and relationships.

We persuaded him to join the Cubs. I was in the Scouts for ten years and learned a great deal about making friends, reading maps and fixing cars. If he could cope, I felt Cubs would be a great place for him to learn a few life skills in a supervised caring environment. The Cub leader was a local mum, and we felt we could explain some of Joe's problems and she would understand his situation. She kept an eye on him, and more importantly, she gave us honest feedback as to how he was doing. We felt confident we could leave him. We hoped he would see how other kids interacted and perhaps he would learn from them. Luckily Joe had a friend from school and they joined up together.

At first I would dread picking Joe up after Cubs. Would I be told he had done something awful? Most nights there wasn't a problem. He would, however, be on a total high, running around like a headless chicken, not wanting to go home. He was by no means the only one, but for Joe it wasn't only letting off steam – he had had a good time and survived. Once in the car he would feel the need to spoil things. This would often happen after a party or successful outing. He was trying to say to us 'I am rubbish. My birth parents got rid of me so I must be. I don't deserve to be successful so I will spoil it.'

We encouraged Joe to go on school and Cub trips and Joy encouraged us to take time off to look after ourselves. Ruth and I needed the breaks; it was something to look forward to and a chance for us to recharge our batteries. We usually travelled a bit, although not too far in case we had to come back quickly. We often stayed in a comfortable city hotel, ate out, drank too much and spent a lot of time in bed doing all the things you can't do when a child is hammering on your bedroom door with a headless Action Man. Without these breaks to look forward to, I do not think we would have made it. It isn't easy to send your adopted son away on a trip; you feel guilty that you are not there to keep him safe, you worry what he might do, what other kids might do to him and what the effect will be on him being away from you. Truth is, in spite of all our reservations, Joe always seemed to have a good time. I think he needed a break from having to sustain a relationship with us as much as we needed a break from him. It was a time for him to relax with people he didn't know so well, and the pressure was off. The only downside of the whole experience was that on his return he would be so tired, after not sleeping properly for four nights, that he would be like a bear with a sore head the whole evening. I sometimes wondered if it was all worth it. But I can tell you it was and is.

Following the work with Joy, Joe found it easier to talk about his past. He would mention things that had happened in his birth family and compare it with his present situation. On our summer holiday, that year, he joined the resort kids' club, and whilst riding an inflatable

81

banana towed at great speed across the bay, he got into conversation with two brothers who were also adopted. On reaching dry land he came and told us all the details. How this subject came up on the banana I have no idea, but it did, and as a result I think he was quite proud to be a member of this exclusive club.

As Joe has got older and matured, his understanding has increased. I think he can deal with the "hows, whats, and wheres" of his past better now. The problem is, he still has a number of negative habits and deep-seated attitudes. To a certain extent, they have kept him safe, but the question is, will he realise they will not help him in the future and will he change or will it be like the alcoholic who only changes when he is at rock bottom? Is it easier for him to carry on as he is? As with so much of our life with Joe, I have absolutely no idea. We have been at it for nine years now, read the books, been on the courses, been through therapy, and I still feel we are where we are more by luck than judgement.

10

Friendship

ED

I hate football. If I had had a son who wanted me to take him to Manchester United every week, this adoption would definitely have broken down halfway through the first football season. Because I work outside, the last thing I feel like doing is riding around on a mountain bike in all weathers in my spare time. I am not a fan of sport in general. Being a more mature parent probably does not help either. I don't think I am an old fart but I am sure Joe does. In fact, I know he does.

When I was growing up, my father didn't spend a lot of time with me, but when it came to friendships, I was not bad. I was never what you would call on the "A list". Those were the cool lads on the Yamaha mopeds with top speeds of 35mph. I was probably on the "B" or "C" list with a Raleigh Wisp, top speed of 25mph downhill with the wind behind me. Trust me – that 10mph difference meant a lot in those days. I had a few good friends, we were not the coolest or the brightest but we were reliable. Ruth might say we were boring. In fact we are so boring we still get together regularly forty years on.

I found it very hard to be Joe's friend. He would say 'I don't like you. You get on my nerves. You are old. You are ugly.' All true statements, but not the real reason he didn't want to be friends. Despite all this I knew I needed to bond with him, but every time I tried to find an activity we could do together, he didn't want to do it. The time I felt we had the most in common was when I read him a story in bed; he loved books. He wasn't too keen on reading, but he loved the stories. When Joe was very young I got fed up with the Postman Pat, Fireman Sam genre, but as he got older, we read *Stig of the Dump* and his favourite, *Just William*. I was always amazed that Joe preferred books with dated language, and odd words even I didn't understand. He admired William's confidence, his ability to convince people to let him run sweet shops by himself or to break into houses to catch robbers. Most of all Joe liked the naughtiness and lawlessness of it all. I sometimes think we may have had less trouble if I had never introduced Joe to William!

I tried to get Joe involved in rowing and canoeing but it was boring or too cold or too wet. I used to cycle a bit when I was young so we would go for a bike ride. He didn't like the hills, he didn't like the route, I was going too slowly or I was going too fast. His deep-seated need for confrontation got in the way of everything we did together, whether it was cycling or making models. I love walking and Joe was never keen at the beginning, but once you got him going he would enjoy it, and could walk for miles. You just had to have a battle first.

Taking refuge in numbers to defuse the conflict, I encouraged Joe to ask a friend to go walking with us. He wasn't very keen but I managed to persuade him and his friend David to climb a local hill. When we left home the weather didn't look too good, and by the time we reached the foot of the hill it was raining quite hard. Luckily David was made of sterner stuff than Joe, and he agreed with me that as we had come this far, we should wrap up well and carry on. So off we went. It was a harder climb than I had thought, so conversation was sparse, but I found myself talking to David more because he was easier to talk to – more relaxed. I had to make an effort to include Joe. I could see that Joe minded David interacting with me, when he either could not or would not. Towards the top of the hill the clouds came down and we couldn't see our hands in front of our faces. Conversation stopped altogether and I sensed Joe was not only uncomfortable, he was getting quite scared. This trip was not going as I had planned. I had imagined the three of us climbing to the top of this hill in warm bright sunshine, looking out at the landscape, and sharing a beautiful experience. Instead Joe was cold, wet and miserable. I had probably succeeded in putting him off walking, alienating him further, and making him dislike David for his ability to relate to other people. Looking back, it was probably not that bad, but at the time it felt that way. When we finally got home, Ruth asked me how I'd got on. What could I say? 'It rained'...I did not say I am no good at all this father and son stuff. He resents me. I don't know why I bother. If he was my birth son we'd have had a natural bond and everything up the hill would have been great. Hell, I bet even the sun would have shone. No, I said: 'It rained'. That was the only thing I was sure about.

As Joe got older, he became easier to get on with. I am keen on cars and I managed to get him to come with me to rallies and shows; he tried to be uninterested but at one show we saw five Bugatti Royales and he was so thrilled with the sheer beauty of the cars that he shot an entire roll of my film to photograph them. I think the fact they were worth a total of sixty million dollars may have impressed him as well. One year we went to the Festival of Speed at Goodwood and I persuaded him to go for a ride in a Paris to Dakar Rally Landrover. His main concern was ruining his hairdo when he put his crash helmet on. He is very

RUTH AND ED ROYCE

interested in his appearance but I am sure that's more of a normal teenager thing.

RUTH
As Joe's behaviour at school improved, his awareness of other children increased but he began to realise he was different. At times this aggravated his loneliness and led to what appeared to be depression – perhaps not full-blown depression, but certainly signs of personal self-doubt.

It was painful to watch him as he struggled to grasp his new world. While his emotional connection to us increased, his connections with his peer group floundered more than ever. The children were used to Joe, the pain in the neck. So, understandably, they were reluctant to accept Joe, who was more bearable but still odd in a different way.

We discussed this with Joy who assured us it was typical, and in a sense normal, for a child with extreme attachment difficulties who was beginning to recover. He would have to go through this process with his peers. She offered to go into the school and talk to the teachers and give them guidance on how they could help Joe. We were in discussions with the school about Joy doing some fun music sessions with Joe and a few of his classmates to help him integrate, when a member of staff told me she had overheard a conversation between some of Joe's peers, which might indicate the music intervention wasn't necessary. Joe was sorting it out on his own, with the help of his friend David.

They had been friends since they were five years old. David also made other friends, Joe didn't, but David always included Joe when he could. The day before, in the playground, this member of staff had heard David defending Joe, telling the other children off, saying, 'He's not so bad now, give him a chance or I'm not playing with you'. So for weeks David played mainly with Joe, until gradually others joined in. Joe started off as the boy nobody wanted much to do with, but through David he became accepted by his classmates as an equal. It seems to me every child needs a David.

I worried that David was doing this only because I was friendly with his mother, Carrie. I mentioned this to Joe's teacher who categorically assured me this wasn't the case. David and Joe genuinely got on; they "clicked", so to speak.

Organising after-school activities to include David was much easier. His calm, quiet humour had a positive effect on Joe's unsteady, flamboyant and more risky character. He seemed to anchor Joe when they played. They complemented each other and had a similar sense of fun.

David usually led their play, not because he was more imaginative than Joe, but because Joe's self-esteem was so low that he was unable to take the initiative. His play was often broken and fragmented and he was unable to sustain the interest of other children. They would intuitively suss out Joe's weaknesses and exploit his failings. But David didn't do that. He accepted Joe's limits, and when Joe did try to exert himself, he didn't exploit his fragility.

Joe had been a peripheral person, edging his way around people, but with David he was himself. Even though Joe had come with a blueprint for rejecting, blaming and hurting other children, here was a child he could trust. He was able to express himself with David, have fights and make up, laugh about nothing and dream about their future plans to travel in a Landrover to Africa, where they would save lives and become heroes!

All through that autumn and the next spring term, Joe grew in confidence. I wouldn't say he was popular, but he was accepted. So school became a more sociable place for him. His friendship with David blossomed, and sleepovers began to happen. Joe loved going to David's house because he had an older sister, two younger brothers and a quiet dad and mum who made him laugh. Carrie exuded love and compassion from every inch of her body, which was quite generous, and mingled in with this was a touch of slightly edgy humour. It was this humour that Joe connected with. He got so much out of his friendship with Carrie and her family. When Carrie drove her four children to the village school, they spilled out of the back of their Landrover, often tripping up as they manoeuvred down the metal step before safely landing with their books and bags. At least one of them would be in a mood, or have thrown an early morning strop, which Carrie would still be sorting out as they made their way to the gate. I always liked her honesty and openness in dealing with her children's many ups and downs. It helped me to feel more normal. They were a magic family for Joe and me. They accepted him for what he was, warts and all. It's all those day-to-day moments, spent together, that counted even more than the therapy sessions, but without Joy's input we would have failed to realise how important these moments were for Joe.

In contrast to these satisfying relationships, his six-monthly visits with his birth brothers were faltering. The fantasy faded a little each time he saw them. He confessed, driving home from one outing, that he had been bored. Friendship was becoming more interesting than brothers he couldn't relate to, because the only thing they shared was their pain.

Joe loved his brothers, and I think that love was reciprocated. The brotherly bond will always exist but there was no working relationship. Their early life had created negative patterns of interaction that hadn't changed. It was frustrating to think there was nothing we could do about it, but all the brothers would need therapy to change the patterns, and that wasn't going to happen. We had to accept it and get on with what we could to improve life for Joe. He was having fun with David and it was a mutually rewarding relationship.

Sadly, in the last year of primary school, when the boys were eleven, David and his family moved to the US. At the time Joe didn't show much emotion, but the first year of secondary school proved to be one of the most challenging for him. It is for many children, but without his friend it was doubly so for Joe. Obviously everything changes eventually, but for a child like Joe, change is something he has had too much of already. He missed David and those years of friendship will always be special for him.

During the first year of secondary school we were constantly reminding Joe that he had made a friend once, so he could do it again. It was and still is a struggle but another friend has come along. This time it's a girl. She has helped Joe survive secondary school but also, I think, helped him to realise that there are lots of people out there who are different and who do not easily fit in.

11

Learning takes off

ED

We always knew Joe was bright. He was naturally keen to learn. When I read to him, he would ask the meaning of any words he didn't understand. Sometimes we would have quite technical conversations and he would show a good grasp of a subject.

I was greatly influenced as a boy by a design engineer who ran the Scouts. From him I learned practical skills, and above all, that if you didn't understand a piece of equipment, you could go away, find out how it worked, take it to bits, and with luck put it together again or even repair it. He showed me that, within reason, anything was possible. He was always ready to have a go. I wanted to pass some of this on to Joe.

On a trip in the car Joe might ask me a question about painting cars. I would tell him about paints in general. Rather than trying to pitch my answer to his level of understanding, and risk talking down to him, I would try to explain as much as I knew, as simply as possible. I worked on the theory that he would get what he could, and perhaps ask about the rest another time. As we went along he would sit and listen intently. Later in the journey something I had said would pop up in conversation, for instance: 'Why doesn't the paint run in the rain?' I could then explain the difference between water-based and oil-based paints. The only problem was that his slightly obsessive nature would kick in, and for the rest of a long journey we would be treated to hours of 'Is that lamp post painted in oil- or water-based paint? Is that fence painted in oil- or water-based paint? Is that gate...? By the time we got to where we were going, I wished I had never told him anything about paint.

When Joe first came to live with us, we visited the local schools and found a slightly untidy but very caring country school run by a motorcycling headmaster. He once described himself to me as a benign dictator. Whilst I was doing a small job for them one afternoon, he came out, pointed to my boots and said, 'Ed, your shoes are undone'. I was instantly whisked back to my first day at school. He was an old style Head, no messing, but very kind. This was just what Joe needed.

With Joy's guidance, the staff worked hard to help Joe over the years he was there, and he changed from a nervous little boy with limited speech clutching his teacher's hand, to a tall, handsome, eloquent lad by the time he left, aged eleven. He still had problems, but when we look back, it is fantastic how much progress he made. Occasionally we would meet professionals who had known Joe in the beginning and who could not believe he was the same person. Because we saw him every day, we couldn't see the changes that were taking place.

RUTH

After therapy with Joy, most people viewed Joe, I think, as slightly quirky but basically a nice kid. He was not aggressive outside the home and now less aggressive at home. Joy gradually became a person of the past. We had a good-bye picnic with her about eighteen months after she finished working with us, when Joe was nine years old. From time to time I would phone her for advice but from Joe's point of view she was no longer in our lives.

This was the most rewarding and satisfying time for Ed and me. I like to think it was the safest, calmest and most fun time of Joe's life. What I observed was a boy who was beginning to get over some of his traumatic experiences and who was feeling safe and learning to trust. However, at the same time Joe developed an attitude. He took up an 'I don't care about myself, I'm a victim, life has done this to me' type of stance. It was as though, as one part of him repaired, another crack emerged. It wasn't one smooth pathway to recovery. There were many diversions that caused us to worry, but nothing like the day-to-day hell we had lived through for the first three years.

Joe made some progress at school. His reading improved slightly and his spelling and writing hardly at all. However, his numerical skills escalated – he loved maths. This was good educationally and very good for his still fragile self-esteem. He was often top of the class and liked the success. He was also very good at puzzles and "thinking" games. We enjoyed doing these with him.

The acquisition of literacy skills was another matter altogether. At the age of eight Joe still struggled to grasp the sounds necessary for reading and spelling and lacked the necessary co-ordination for writing. He could narrate a brilliant, imaginative story for me to write down, but he wouldn't even try to write it himself. People assured us this was a "boy thing". I wasn't convinced.

Like all parents, it was important for us to have some positive feedback. Everyone needs a pat on the back. I think it was in Year Four or Five, when he was eight or nine, Joe came home with a painting of a girl in the style of an artist called Lichtenstein. I'm no expert on art, but this painting was different from his other work. The colours were brighter, it was clearly defined and the entire picture was well formed. Previously his drawings had made some kind of reference to trauma in his past life: people dissected, scenes broken into sections, and always in dark colours. They were fragmented and unpleasing to look at, but this portrait was open, cheerful and a pleasure to see. I wondered if he had done it on his own and he looked surprised I should ask. Of course he had done it all on his own!

Many teachers told us Joe was bright, but when your child can't read, write and spell like other children, you do wonder if they know what they are talking about. Joe couldn't do things his peer group could do. The frustration for him was intense and for us bewildering, until one day I was given some handouts on a training day organised by Adoption UK. That was when I realised the teachers did know what they were talking about. Joe asked me to read him one of the handouts. It was a poem. It went like this.

Not flesh of my flesh
Nor bone of my bone
But still miraculously my own
Never forget for a single minute
You didn't grow under my heart
But in it!
Anon.

He couldn't read it himself, of course, but he understood it immediately. 'That's a forever Mum not a birth Mum saying that!' he blurted out.

One evening I was watching the *Tonight* programme. It was about a new cure for dyslexia being offered by an organisation called DORE (Developing Skills for Life). Many of the symptoms they described were similar to Joe's difficulties. I looked into it and decided to arrange an assessment. They confirmed that Joe had dyslexia.

The village school Joe attended was very supportive and quite innovative in its approach to education. They were willing to give anything a try if it benefited the child. So the DORE programme was not seen as a threat but as an opportunity.

I could see how much Joe's poor reading and spelling affected his self-esteem and considered that reason enough to put him through the programme. When I told Joy about it, she thought Joe and I doing exercises together, which required co-operation from Joe and leadership from me, would do his attachment a power of good. Joe was motivated because he wanted to read, so he worked exceptionally hard doing his exercises every morning before school and every afternoon when we got back. After three months of grind, he began to see results. His reading became more fluent and he could concentrate for longer. He was getting satisfaction from reading rather than finding it a chore, but his spelling didn't improve.

After six months Joe lost interest; we kept it going for the full twelve months, albeit with less enthusiasm. According to DORE, after one year on the programme, the cerebellum part of Joe's brain was functioning as it should, but his eye movements were still erratic, so that he was inclined to lose track of the words.

Joe's weekly treat after school on a Friday was to buy the *Beano* comic. Up until then he had merely glanced at the pictures, but with his new ability he would sit in the car unable to drag himself away from Dennis, Gnasher and the Numskulls, while I went into the kitchen to prepare tea. He was totally absorbed in it. It was wonderful to see him enjoy himself like other children.

Another of Joe's remaining problems was his poor ability in relation to time, space and distance. Here was a clever boy who still didn't know which house, village, county or country he lived in when he was nine years old. He had absolutely no idea which town we went shopping in. Once when Ed took him to a swimming lesson, he unwittingly drove to the wrong town. Joe genuinely did not recognise any landmarks for the entire 10-mile journey. Sometimes during the weekend or holidays he would ask if it was dinnertime yet when we had only just finished breakfast. He had no awareness of the time of day or day of the week. Even now, aged thirteen, he doesn't know the months of the year in spite of his high IQ. All these things may sound trivial. They would be if they were isolated symptoms, but for Joe they were another barrier to learning and feeling safe.

Joe's education was linked to how he felt about himself. Until he felt securely attached to an adult, he was unable to let his head absorb knowledge because he was preoccupied with keeping himself safe. Learning requires finding out about something new, something you don't know. Infants learn to deal with new experiences through trusting someone else. If they don't have anyone to trust, they are unable to learn as effectively as they should. It took Joe a long time to change this infant pattern.

Joe had always enjoyed listening to me play the piano (not very well). So I asked if he would like to learn. He was keen. I knew that learning through trial and error would be challenging for him, but decided we would give it a go. He learnt for nearly two years, making good progress and showed some musical talent. However, his main achievement was dealing with failure. He learnt that if you fail initially but try again and again, you can succeed. This was something he hadn't experienced before. It gave him confidence and taught him perseverance. He gave up learning the piano because he didn't want to do exams and wasn't committed enough to do the practice, but not because he was afraid to fail.

The school reports, as Joe went up through primary school, were a joy to read. He loved structured classroom teaching, was well behaved and had friends. What more could we ask for? We made much fuss of him, as did his teachers.

Joe's anxiety did not magically go away. He developed severe headaches when he was about nine years old, usually going very pale and needing to lie down. The optician prescribed mild glasses to re-align his sight but the problem persisted. A scan revealed no obvious cause; the paediatrician considered that the trauma in his early life could have caused developmental damage to the immature brain, and could well be the cause of his headaches.

Obsessive habits became another worry. Joe would blink excessively when stressed, he constantly rearranged his clothes and he had a mild tic from time to time. We read up a lot about obsessive behaviours and decided the best approach was to talk to Joe ourselves and help him de-stress. I told him about my own habit, when I was a child competing in swimming galas. I would go through a ritual of movements as I stood on the starting block, feeling it imperative that each side of my body was equal as I shuffled about, otherwise I wouldn't win. He listened and gradually the habits faded.

There were times we thought Joe had slight autistic tendencies but we put that one on the back burner when, from reading the research, we realised that most people have them to some degree. It's a matter of where you fit on the spectrum and Joe was probably not much higher than average.

Joe's attitude of "I'm a victim" grew into "I take no responsibility for my life" and caused problems from time to time. I heard other children telling Joe to take the blame rather than deny something that was so blatantly his doing. But blame had much greater significance for him than for other children. Blame goes to the core of who you are, and if you don't know who you are, how can you deal with it? You don't, you transfer it to someone or something else. The dog was often the culprit in Joe's case. Sometimes even objects would be blamed, like a table for knocking over a glass of milk, or a shoe for bringing stones into the house. This was baffling to us because it defied all logic. This sort of behaviour introduced a chaotic element into our home. Joe liked the feeling of living in chaos. Chaos was familiar to him. He still sometimes preferred the old feelings he recognised to the new feelings of calm and contentment.

In the end, learning took off because Joe gradually became anchored and felt safe. He was able to use his head for thinking and allow himself to be totally absorbed rather than on the look-out for the next threat. Fear no longer dominated his brain, his life or our lives.

12

On holiday

RUTH

Before therapy we had felt Joe wouldn't cope with a journey to New Zealand to see my dad, but he was calmer now, so we decided to risk our hard-earned savings for what could be four weeks of family fun or twenty-eight days of holiday hell.

He had met my father and two cousins when they were on holiday here in the UK. It was time, we decided, for him to meet more of my relations and see that I had a family too, albeit 12,000 miles away. We wanted to make the trip more of an adventure by stopping off in a few places on the way there and while coming back. We also planned to tour the North Island calling in on scattered family or, as Ed called it, go relative-bashing.

The stopover in Singapore was exciting for us all, especially Joe who discovered egg fried rice and swimming pools with real palm trees. At the hotel, a glass-bottomed swimming pool that revealed the swimmers' dangling legs under the water particularly appealed to him. The Buddhist and Hindu temples, as you would expect, generated less excitement.

Joe soaked up all the vibrant sounds, smells and colours; he did not feel menaced, as we had feared he might do. During our few days in Singapore he became more compliant than ever, usually doing what he was asked immediately. We felt more together here than we ever had at home. This togetherness gathered even more momentum in New Zealand as we drove down the North Island avoiding the sulphur city of Rotorua, admiring the volcanoes, and digesting the vast, endless, gentle farmlands before arriving at my father's home. Even though Joe had the added pressure of fitting into my father's unfamiliar routine, he adapted and attached himself to Cleopatra the cat, spending hours outside stroking her while basking in the warm January sunshine.

The cat was a clever strategy. Joe lay low with her until he felt safe in this new place. At least he was motivated to fit in, which was a huge improvement from his early days with us. He loved the big blue skies, the space to ride his bike and the relaxed way of living.

Joe enjoyed playing on the street and his daily job of cycling on the footpaths (there were very few pedestrians, in fact there were very few people anywhere) by himself to the fruit and vegetable farm shop. He was very insistent that only one item could be purchased per ride, and so he took over an hour, cycling backwards and forwards, just so that we could assemble a salad for lunch. He liked the freedom as well as the control, of course.

One day, after about a week at my father's house, I decided to leave Joe at the local swimming baths on his own for an hour while I went back for afternoon tea with my father. This was a huge step for both of us, but it was a small town with only a few children swimming, and the pool was well supervised. Joe had been approached by some of the children and played with them for a while but they had soon lost interest in him apart from one little Maori boy. I overheard this child say to Joe, 'What's ya name, English boy?' I looked back to see Joe going with him to what I recognised as the most hallowed part of the outdoor baths. I hoped Joe wouldn't ask awkward questions because this strip of tarmac, I remembered from my childhood, was special and a privilege to lie on. It was covered in towels warming up in the sun, ready for when the children came out of the water. Joe still lacked the spontaneity most children have when they meet new children. He often looked quite robotic and totally ill at ease as he tried to figure out how to behave. But the Maori lad was oblivious to Joe's problems and just took charge.

The journey around the North Island was interspersed with visits to local swimming baths and visiting family. We then made our way back to Auckland for the flight to Sydney and then Bangkok. While in New Zealand, I noticed many changes in my relatives. All of them were older (of course!), some fatter, and some wealthier while others were stuck in a rut. Most of them meant little to me, they were distant relations from my childhood, but one in particular stood out. He made a small gesture, a sort of wave of his hand across his face, indicating shyness. He had made that same gesture as a young man. Living 12,000 miles away from my family, I had not remembered the importance of all those family traits that make up your identity; some were ghastly and best forgotten, but others gave a sense of pride and worth.

I recall looking at Joe and thinking 'you aren't growing up with these family traits and you don't look like any of your adoptive family'. Adopted children suffer a permanent loss, no matter which way you look at it. They lose all their family attributes. An added confusion for children like Joe is that many of their family's characteristics aren't exactly ones to be proud of, making the loss even more difficult and complex to deal with.

As we flew out of Auckland, and I thought of Joe's losses, I felt my own loss and separation more acutely than ever before. Over the years I had come to terms with my decision to live in England. I chose, as an adult, to live away from my family. But Joe's separation was forced upon him and must be made a million times worse by his limited experience and perception. I couldn't imagine the pain he must sometimes feel.

A few days before we left New Zealand I was showing Joe a "hongi", a Maori kiss. We were pressing our noses together and I explained to him about "ha" or "breath of life", which is exchanged and intermingled when kissing like this. I told him that for many Maori people it is a serious gesture or greeting representing 'the essence of life for human kind; where the breath of life enters us'. Joe soaked up information of this kind, but for me the symbolism of rubbing noses was significant. Only a few days after this, while in Australia, Joe started to kiss me rather than giving me the usual brush of the cheeks. I know it sounds like small stuff to other parents, but it was life-changing for both of us. Four years earlier I wouldn't have believed it possible.

We stayed in Australia for a few days enjoying all the sights of Sydney and the Hunter Valley before flying to Thailand for a final week's holiday.

ED

When Ruth said she wanted us to go to New Zealand as a family, I was not very keen. We had been abroad but never on such a long distance flight. Joe always looked forward to flying, but after take-off his interest would wane and he would start to fidget. The timing of the flight was crucial. We wanted to get to the airport around seven pm, feed him, tuck him up in a dark corner of the terminal and get him to go to sleep. When it was time to board, we would carry him on half asleep, and with a bit of luck he would stay asleep through most of the flight. If all went according to plan, he would wake up in time for a meal, a film and the landing.

Joe was keen to travel but there could be problems if he became stressed. He had a heightened sense of smell and hearing. Environments that wouldn't bother us could be overwhelming for him, and make him react badly and be aggressive. We once took him to a bird market in a foreign city. To begin with he was fascinated by the various brightly coloured species; as we went deeper in, he was overpowered by the noise and stimulation. He became aggressive, turned and ran out. Eventually we found him and took him somewhere quiet until he calmed down.

It was not so easy to calm him down on a plane. When we landed at Bangkok, there was a long delay before we could disembark. We all sat there for an hour-and-a-half with no air-conditioning, getting hotter and hotter. Joe got more and more uncomfortable. He started shouting and kicking the seats in front of him, to everyone's annoyance. When Joe gets uncomfortable and stressed, he just lets go. At a talk I went to recently, the speaker said that the part of the brain that regulates anger also regulates stress, and is often underdeveloped in children with attachment disorder. This goes a long way to explain the link between Joe's stress and anger and his inability to cope in uncomfortable situations. Back on the plane we gave him a drink, took most of his clothes off, and luckily that soothed him considerably. But I was glad to get off, and glad I would probably never see any of my fellow passengers again.

Joe loved staying in hotels and the posher the better. For obvious reasons we didn't stay in establishments that were too upmarket. Joe always rated the smartness of the doorman. One doorman had gold ropes and tassels on his uniform and Joe thought this must be the best hotel in town. On arrival he always tested the beds by jumping from one to the other and then noted the range of nuts and sweets in the mini-bar. His inspection of the room would finish with an in-depth examination of all the TV channels;

he was often disappointed to find, in the words of Bruce Springsteen, '57 channels and nothing on', especially if most of the programmes were in a foreign language.

We never ate in the hotels. After checking out the swimming pool, we would look for food. Joe was not a fan of gourmet food and I was not a fan of hotel prices. We would usually go out and find a local café. In Bangkok we frequented the next-door greasy spoon where Joe was most impressed by the roast ducks, complete with heads, hanging above the counter. He would always have his usual: a bowl of egg fried rice and a steaming mug of hot chocolate.

We organised a ride on a long-tailed boat, but just as we were about to board, Joe got very upset. We didn't know what the problem was. On reflection I can see that the heat, the smell from the river and the noise of the engine were just too much for him. We had to learn to watch for signs that Joe was struggling. One evening we went to an outdoor market piled high with food, all the colours of the rainbow. All sorts of fish and meat were cooking and there were people everywhere. It was an overpowering experience, but by dipping in and out of the market and finding quiet places every now and then, we found we could stop Joe from getting stressed. I think in some ways this was a crude form of cognitive therapy, a bit like acclimatising guide dogs to busy streets. By taking Joe to stimulating places I think we desensitised him, and helped him to survive stressful situations, as Joy had taught him to do.

When we told people that we intended to fly to New Zealand with Joe, many of them advised us not to attempt such a long trip. I'm afraid some people thought exposing Joe to these experiences was almost abusive. Looking back, I am sure that we were giving him confidence to cope in the future, out in the real world.

13

Are we mad?

ED

Right from the start of this adoption business Ruth wanted two children; I was not that fussed. We would have adopted a second child earlier if Joe hadn't caused such disruption in our lives. With the best will in the world, during the first few years we would have struggled to cope with a well-behaved rabbit, let alone another adopted child. The trouble was the clock was ticking. Not so much Ruth's biological clock, because that stopped a long time ago, but we were getting older and more knackered. I was conscious while waiting at the school gate that I looked more like Joe's granddad than his father. Joe always takes great pleasure in telling me how wrinkly I am. Having challenging kids is something best done when you are reasonably young and fit.

We'd had a rough few years and with a bit of luck life was improving. Perhaps in the future, if things calmed down, we would have a bit more money to spare and could do a few of the things we had planned to do if we didn't adopt again. Been there, done that, got the T-shirt. Ruth's point, and I could understand it, was that although Joe was making progress, he wasn't being helped by being an only child. He was becoming very self-centred and selfish. Because he was so needy, he demanded, and for the most part got, our undivided attention. If we adopted another child, Joe would have to share us; problem was, would this undo all the good work we had done so far with him? But there was going to come a point in Joe's life when he would have to share and he would not be the centre of attention, so it might as well be now.

Ruth felt that over the years we had built up a lot of knowledge and expertise that would be wasted if we didn't adopt again. I could have lived with that, but once we decided to go ahead and adopt again, I put all the worries and "what ifs" to the back of my mind, as I had done with Joe.

RUTH

Originally we had been approved for two children, so having another child seemed the next step for us. We ran the idea past Joe who, like most ten-year-olds, was keen on the idea of another child living with him. At this stage we didn't involve him too much as it had to be our decision, not his.

In the summer of 2004 we contacted our local authority adoption team and two other adoption agencies; the Catholic Society, NCH and Emma from our local authority visited us. They were all very efficient, giving us information to read and consider so we could decide if they were the right agency for us. Gut instinct told us to go with someone we knew and trusted, so we opted for our local social services department because we liked Emma and could work with her. She agreed with her line manager on a shortened assessment that wouldn't go over old ground. This assessment focused on us now, as a family, and on the impact that adoption would have on Joe and the kind of relationship he might have with another child. All the statutory procedures were followed regarding references, police checks, health checks, and our financial situation.

The assessment started in July and was ready for panel by November. In the meantime, Emma contacted a colleague in the same department about a boy who needed an adoptive placement. This social worker made a speedy entrance into our lives, keen to secure a placement for Jack, who was seven-and-a-half years old.

ED

The home visits were much easier this time: I knew and liked Emma. Everything went very smoothly. Social services came up with a seven-year-old lad who seemed pleasant. We visited him and got on well together. He appeared to be interested in the things I was interested in. He was quite fun. It all seemed fine to me. Ruth was not so sure, she had seen more of him than me; she had been on more visits. Through her work she had experience of children like Jack when they were older. She kept saying to me: 'He has learning difficulties, he is very manipulative, he obviously struggles to read and write. Are you prepared for the future if he can't survive in the outside world? Are you prepared to look after him when he is an adult?' We had always been adamant that we did not want to be caring for someone until we die. Jack seemed fairly straightforward to me, although I could see he had a learning problem. If you told him the names of things, he would not remember five minutes later. But surely, after all those years at school, he would be able to read enough to drive a van and earn a living; it was not as if we wanted him to go to university. I told myself: we have made the decision to adopt a second child. I liked Jack. There are no guarantees with any child. Let's get on with it. Ruth was not so sure.

RUTH

We wanted a boy between the ages of seven and nine, who

would have contact with siblings. We did not feel we could cope with a disability, but could manage a diagnosed learning difficulty. We definitely wanted a child who had the capacity to make attachments easily. The latter was by far the most important for us, given our experience with Joe. So when we were presented with information about Jack, we asked to see the psychologist's assessment. This reassured us with phrases like "good sense of self". However, we felt we needed more information, so requested social services to pay Joy to make an assessment. This might sound like we were putting Jack through a test to see if he was "fit for purpose", but we felt we needed to be sure. A lot was at stake.

Social services agreed, and once again we went to Bristol, this time to look at the video Joy had made during her assessment. Joy noted many positive signs in relation to attachment: Jack showed an appropriate level of anxiety when left with her by his social worker, and he made good eye contact. But she also drew our attention to his exceptionally poor concentration. And he produced a drawing during the assessment of his foster family with a speech bubble saying "help". Later I was to realise the full significance of that.

Jack is one of a large sibling group. He was to have face-to-face contact with one brother, and an annual exchange of letters with the others as well as with his birth mother. He had learning difficulties but was quite able to attend mainstream school. Looking back, it's odd that we laid such importance on both boys having the same type of contact. We considered it would be healthier, more equal and easier to manage. Adults have a knack of assuming something is an issue for a child when it is of no importance to them.

It was a rollercoaster ride for us all; Joe was very excited to begin with although he showed some reservations, or perhaps disappointment would be more accurate, when he met Jack during the introductions. Jack was particularly small for his age, and quite delayed in many areas of his development. We noticed it too, of course, but put it down to the neglect and upheaval in his early life. Ed and Jack clicked, so to speak, immediately they met. Jack fired back a witty response to Ed in that "lads together" sort of way. I was less charmed and more intrigued by his willingness to let everybody do everything for him. We were approved and matched with Jack at the beginning of November and he moved in on the 30th.

During week two of the placement I showed him one of Joe's old books. It was *Spot the Dog*, a book most five- or six-year-olds would romp through. Jack struggled to turn the pages, never mind read them. He appeared not to understand the concept of reading at all, claiming no one had ever read him a story before. He was reluctant to sit and listen, and unable to sustain concentration long enough to wait for the end. At the same time, the school was querying his test results provided by his previous school. We thought it was probably the shock of moving, as did his teacher.

In the meantime, Joe, quite understandably, was struggling with sharing us, especially me. After the first few months, his old aggressive habits started to resurface. We recognised that Jack was stirring up feelings about his birth brothers. Eventually, one evening Joe burst into tears saying we sided with Jack all the time and he was blamed for everything. I was pleased in one way, because crying was far more normal than his increasing aggression, but sadly his view of Jack was deteriorating. Joe felt he was being pushed into the role of scapegoat again, just as he had been by his birth brothers, while unbeknown to us, Jack was busy re-enacting his role of helpless victim and family snitch.

The two boys spent two terms at the same primary school and it did not go well. What followed is what I can only describe as the summer holidays from hell. By the end of August, I handed in my notice at work, because although it was only part-time, I was feeling exhausted and Ed was tired of the hassle from two boys who did not like each other.

ED

After Jack moved in, I always felt Ruth slightly resented him. I am not sure whether she felt that he would be responsible for taking away any chance of an enjoyable old age, or that we had been pushed into agreeing to go ahead when we were not ready. We both knew that Jack had a lot of problems, but we didn't know exactly what they were. We tried to find answers by involving various experts who came up with assorted theories but no one seemed to have the definitive answer.

Ruth saw much more of Jack than I did. I would see him after work and at weekends, but she had the day-to-day care. Joe would often swear at me but Jack never did. He was more likely to say things behind my back or to tell tales about me. If you did things for him, he was usually appreciative. At Christmas and birthdays he was thrilled with his presents, something Joe never was. It made a nice change not to be told that you had got it wrong again (it was not what he wanted and you should have known better). Jack had a fair bit of empathy; if you were sick he would bring you a cuddly toy or make a card. He had worked out that being nice to people was more productive than being nasty.

At the beginning, I tended only to see Jack's good points. I either could not see behind his cheerful mask or I chose not to. It seemed to me Ruth was worrying too much.

RUTH

Sometime during the summer months an inspector visited

us from the Social Services Inspectorate because they were assessing our local authority adoption agency. As Jack was a new placement, they asked to visit us at home. It was straightforward from our point of view but the boys had an interesting reaction. For the first time in months, they played beautifully together in the sandpit for the entire duration of the visit. Even after six years, Joe felt menaced by an official coming to our home. Jack, it seemed, liked us enough to be motivated to make a good impression.

The one common factor in the boys' lives was their dread of going back into foster care. Perhaps they thought this inspector might cart them off to another foster home. So, after eight months, the boys' relationship seemed to hinge on a shared fear. They appeared to have nothing else in common. Joe was a bright eleven-year-old, achieving well at school, slowly establishing a friendship group, keen to have a go at anything, relishing new skills, developing independence with an increasingly positive view of himself. Jack was not doing well at school, learning was a threat to him and something to resist, he had lots of "mates" but was unable to distinguish real friendship, he thrived on dependence and lacked self-esteem; in short, he saw himself as a person who needed help because he was essentially a helpless victim.

As Joe's relationship with Jack worsened, I felt myself empathising with Joe. He came home from school one day and asked me to come into the living room. We sat on the sofa, and with a very serious face he asked me, did we realise we were adopting the dumbest kid in the school? Jack couldn't do anything; even Danny (a boy with Down's syndrome) could do more than Jack. I thanked him for his concern and assured him we knew what we were doing. Six months later, I wasn't so sure.

In the autumn term his teacher and Ed and I expressed real concerns about Jack's achievement at school. The results of his tests eighteen months earlier didn't match what he was able to do now. And although all the upheaval of moving from his family to foster care and then to us would have caused him to regress, it didn't add up to what he was currently achieving or rather, not achieving.

At home we were noticing how simple domestic tasks were a challenge for him. Unfortunately, his year in foster care had failed to teach him to clean his teeth, to go to the toilet without making a mess and he was unable to wash himself in the bath. His eating habits were a problem too: he couldn't hold a knife and fork or chew his food; the mess on the floor after a meal looked like it had been made by a baby in a high chair.

After a year with us, when he was nearly nine, we realised that, in fact, we were living with a six-year-old on a good day and a four-year-old on a bad one.

All this time, Emma was in the background offering advice and support. She never criticised our doubts and delays, just listened. Unfortunately, some of her colleagues weren't quite so professional. Jack's social worker, like so many social workers who are responsible for children, had little understanding or experience of adoption.

She also knew very little about Jack because he was one of a large sibling group where he had faded into the background. She admitted that he was like a little boy lost; nobody really knew him. How on earth could they talk about matching when little or nothing was known about one half of the match?

A number of professionals provided advice. The general consensus was that Jack was a boy of low ability although his verbal reasoning skills were average, meaning he could be articulate. This was masking his weaker cognitive skills. His inability to perceive a sequence was of particular concern. He was unable to put words or numbers in order and had no understanding of the value of a number.

I was having doubts about Jack. He was very affectionate but in a pussycat sort of way: stroking me, purring up to my legs and clinging to me like a lost little kitten. He was such a sweet, docile little boy with a big grin but there was something very superficial about him. Joe's pain was out in the open, whereas Jack's pain was masked by his clown act, and to some degree, by his learning disability.

Jack's social worker was pressuring us to proceed with the adoption. His younger brother, who had been placed after Jack, had already been adopted. I dreaded the review meetings when half a dozen officials would sit in our house talking about Jack, a child they knew almost nothing about. Their view was based on theories, and as Ed reminded them on one occasion, 'This is a job for you, but this is my family's life, so don't start dictating to me when I should sign up for taking responsibility for another person's life'.

ED

Regularly, throughout this period, I would have to take time off work when gangs of social workers, Independent Reviewing Officers, various secretaries and assorted trainees would occupy all the available chairs in our kitchen. They would drink our tea and discuss the adoption progress. At first it was very much 'if you are not ready you do not have to decide', but as time went on, I felt we were being bullied into setting a date for the adoption. At one point a social worker suggested they could take Jack away if we did not agree to adopt him. I said we would not be threatened.

But we had come too far to go back, and I felt we had to adopt Jack. When I said this to Ruth, she said I didn't appreciate what we would be getting into, which was probably true, but I could not see that we had any alternative.

RUTH

The nagging doubts wouldn't go away, so in the autumn, a

few days after Jack went back to school, I confided in Emma. She was very understanding. We talked for ages and agreed that the adoption didn't have a chance of working if we didn't feel right. I remember we talked about his foster placement and how unhappy he had been there. The drawing he did for Joy with the "help" bubble clearly showed his feelings. But it wasn't 'Help! My foster carers are horrid people', it was, 'Help! I'm a helpless person who hides, disguises and deceives. I'm the lost little boy whom nobody knows.'

Emma said, 'If you were prepared to travel all the way to Bristol for Joe, then perhaps you should consider the same for Jack. He obviously needs some help in making new relationships and becoming part of your family.'

So I made an appointment for us to see Joy.

14

Form-storm-norm-perform

RUTH

A friend of mine said to me that "Form-storm-norm-perform" was a theory she used in basic training for youth workers. Apparently, every new group goes through this process, so according to her, our family would do the same. Why should we be any different? It would be odd if there were no ripples, waves or even a tsunami from time to time but eventually calm would return and we would be a family. I was hoping Joy could create waves and even a tsunami because by this stage I was thoroughly fed up with living with a clown, and a kitten with a passion for nuzzling my left leg.

Jack had many habits that bothered me; not getting to sleep and remaining asleep was one of them. Quite understandable, given that his first seven years of sleep had been spent frightened, wet, dirty and interrupted. Unsafe and scared, bedtime had meant red alert time for him. He would be up and down until he fell asleep exhausted. Often he was still wandering around at eleven o'clock when we were going to bed. His behaviour at school reflected his growing fatigue. We were told schoolteachers had provided him with a beanbag to sleep on when he lived with his birth family, and they had given him bananas to boost his energy level. So he had learnt to live with tiredness. Now he was becoming increasingly distressed by it. He wanted to change but his tiny body wasn't letting him.

When we saw the community paediatrician for Jack's annual check-up at the beginning of his third year with us (because we hadn't yet adopted him he was technically still a child "in care"), I mentioned the sleep problem. Up until now our focus had been on decaying teeth, poor co-ordination and learning difficulties. During the discussion I said that his sleep pattern improved slightly in the autumn because it got darker earlier. She said immediately: 'Melatonin, he's got a melatonin problem'.

Three days later, the local pharmacist obtained melatonin for us. Jack's brain switched off within fifteen minutes of the bedroom light going off. It was like a miracle. Within a week he was sleeping deeply. And guess what, his behaviour at school improved, especially his concentration! Until then I had not comprehended the impact sleep deprivation can have on a child. I still wonder how much of Jack's learning disability can be attributed to seven years of disrupted uncomfortable sleep.

That previous summer we had ventured to Italy for a holiday. One incident at the camping ground illustrated why Jack had such difficulties with Joe. I told Jack to go to the toilet and come straight out to where I was waiting for him. He was at that awkward age when he didn't want to go into the ladies but I wasn't entirely confident about him going into the men's alone. So I guided him to the door of the nearest cubicle and waited outside perched on a bench within earshot and sight of the toilet block, until I heard this almighty scream. I knew it was Jack.

I rushed to the entrance and was greeted by a confused

looking Frenchman; the cubicle door was shaking violently. There was utter panic in Jack's voice. The Frenchman sensed it too, and immediately clambered into the next cubicle and endeavoured to calm him. I was outside the door trying to talk him down. But he was hysterical. The Frenchman was bewildered and gave me odd looks. Why was the boy so frantic and why was I on the verge of tears?

Somehow the door unlocked itself. Jack flew out. I ran after him, shouting 'Thank you' to my gallant Gallic friend. But Jack was gone. Now I panicked; this was a big site and not the sort of place an upset nine-year-old with learning disabilities should be roaming around at nine-thirty at night. I was just about to head back to fetch Ed when I spotted him. He was sitting alone under a tree.

In the past Jack had talked about his family, but I always felt he told everyone these same stories as a way of getting attention from social workers. He knew they liked to hear that sort of stuff. But this time it was different. The distress was evident as he held on to me.

He told me that his brothers used to lock him in the loo. He spent many nights sleeping on the floor of the toilet. In a normal house this would be bad enough, but this was a household where there was quite literally shit up to the ceiling. So for Jack it meant spending a night on damp urine-soaked flooring smeared in faeces. They wouldn't let him out, and it happened on more than one occasion.

I thanked him for telling me and said he was brave. I didn't know what else to say. But it bought home to me how his parents' failure to keep his older brothers under control had deeply hurt Jack, and this had affected his relationship with Joe. Not surprisingly, he's not big on trusting other children.

I realised too, that I did care about Jack, quite a lot more than I had thought. His vulnerabilities were not as obvious as Joe's but nevertheless still there. Jack's early years had been spent in deceiving adults, telling lies for his father and spying on his siblings. He had a preference for telling tales – that Joe had given him forbidden sweets, or was planning a midnight feast – because he didn't understand that Joe was trying to be matey with him. He saw Joe's attempts at friendship as an opportunity to get special attention from us, to be our spy and conspire with us. We, as well as the social workers, were naïve to think that a boy with so many difficulties with his own birth siblings was going to have fewer problems with a sibling by adoption, especially one with issues of his own.

ED

One summer we had a family holiday in Sienna during the horse race week and the place was heaving. We were walking down the main street watching the crowds and looking in all the shop windows. After five minutes I looked around for Jack but he had disappeared. We searched through the crowds with no luck. I started to retrace my steps, checking all the shops. We eventually found him in a toyshop; he had just walked in and had no idea of the problem he had caused. No matter how many times I told him to stay close, he would run off or walk into a shop without telling anyone. Twice during that holiday he ran out into the road in front of a car that had to screech to a stop to avoid hitting him. I could see the Italian drivers looking at me and thinking: 'That irresponsible father can't look after his child'. I spent most of that holiday holding his hand like a toddler. Jack didn't like it but it was the only way to keep him safe. Ruth spent most of that holiday saying to me, 'Now you know what he is like...'

It was only when I was with Jack all day for two weeks that I realised the size of the problem. I was at a loss to understand his educational difficulties too. I would hear him read in the evenings and he would struggle to read the same word over and over on every line in the book. No matter how many times you told him what it was, he could not remember it next time. I was convinced he was playing games, trying to get out of reading by making me so exasperated that I would give up and let him watch television. The school was having the same problem and putting it down to lack of self-esteem and security in his past life.

We were in agreement that there was a problem with Jack that we did not understand and that we had not been told about. Ruth wanted something done, some sort of provision made for the future, and would not agree to legally adopt Joe until we had this in place. The trouble was that we were the only people who thought there was a serious problem, and we didn't know what to do about it; neither did the social workers.

So back to Joy.

RUTH

Joy knew Jack from the assessment prior to coming to us. So when the four of us rolled up one Saturday afternoon, introductions weren't necessary. Like Joe, Jack immediately related to her, but unlike Joe, he also immediately co-operated with her, following instructions and completing tasks set for him. There was no lone mountaineer struggling to conquer his Everest draped in musical instruments and ignoring any offer of help this time. Jack included us. It was all very cosy until Joy sat him down and said to him, 'You're not as thick as you pretend, are you Jack?' He did his usual cute little kitten smile. She persisted. 'You worked out that, if you pretend to be thick, other people will do it for you. Am I right?'

No response from Jack, but he was looking uncomfortable.

Joy said that she knew he wasn't thick because he had just successfully completed a set of tasks that required a person to use their brain. If he were as thick as he pretended to be, he wouldn't be able to do that. 'I know he doesn't find reading and numbers easy, but people who find those things difficult aren't necessarily thick and stupid'. He was a fake! As she said this she paused, and then glanced at him. Jack started to giggle. 'I'm right, aren't I, Jack?' He laughed more and more, so much so, he rolled off the sofa onto the floor nodding his head. He said 'yes' through giggles as he rolled around. She had caught him out and he knew it.

Joy then went on to explain that Jack had developed a mask to protect himself. This mask hid the real Jack; what we were getting was 'I'm thick and helpless but a jolly clown'.

Jack and I spent the next few months visiting Joy and her colleague Kate, an art therapist. During this time Jack drew many pictures of himself, starting off with a bland happy face, but ending six months later with an "I dunno" face, a sad face, and a clever face. None of this was perhaps revolutionary but it showed that Jack now accepted that he was more than a thick jolly little boy. It was the beginning of feeling he was worthy of being a person in his own right. Alongside this newfound sense of who he was came the darker side of Jack. Stomping of feet, slamming of doors and 'no' entered his repertoire. He would actually spell it out: N-O!

The following Easter, Jack won the trophy for the junior who had made most progress that term. The mask he had hidden behind for so long was coming off and freeing up his brain to do some thinking. I'm not suggesting his learning difficulties disappeared. Of course they didn't, but his motivation to have a go, his belief in himself, and his capacity to be a whole person emerged.

While Jack was seeing Joy, Joe's behaviour at home had deteriorated dramatically since going to secondary school. He was bullied in Year 7 and was struggling to make relationships. His somewhat eccentric behaviour set him apart from his peers. Added to this was his size. He grew six centimetres in six months and experienced all the physical changes of a sixteen-year-old. While he was not disruptive in class, his aggression at home increased. When Joe had these aggressive outbursts, he would later dissociate from them completely, denying all knowledge that they had ever taken place. He never hit us – he knew that would be one step too far. Instead he targeted our belongings.

Joe blamed us for his "posh voice" and his lack of "street cred". He was convinced he would have been happier running around playing football, a member of the gang. These discussions usually developed on the drive home from the school bus stop. One day he admitted that he could have become a thug type of guy because he had been so wild and out of control when he was younger; he examined himself with such honesty and integrity. He was going to be all right. He was not going to turn into some mass murderer, as I had once feared. And although Jack's presence was a challenge for him, he would have had to grapple with these kinds of issues at some point. Jack had just brought them forward.

During the Easter holidays, when Jack had been seeing Joy for three months, the boys were playing with some other children and for the first time I heard Joe defend Jack. It was music to my ears. I could have cried but didn't, because true to role, Jack was soon in the kitchen moaning about someone else. But at last we were making progress. We were moving out of the storm and our life was beginning to take on a degree of normality.

Jack and Joe were both changing so much at this time. We were excited and exhausted. More than two years of fighting, whinging and living in a war zone once more had taken its toll on Ed and me.

When we went to the US to visit Joe's friend David and his family, an overly made-up Bostonian lady, draped in gold and wrapped up in a mink coat, looked at our two in the hotel lift and said, 'You are two Christmas angels'. We all kept a straight face until we erupted into laughter in the corridor. I don't know if the boys picked up the irony of this lady's comments, but it was the first time we all really laughed together. We made our way out into the Boston snow, united as a family. These moments don't happen very often for us, so it's a matter of making the most of them when they do. The angel lady gave us the best present ever. We felt together and we were having fun.

Joy's work with Jack led to our acceptance of his disability and, at the same time, gave us permission to expect more, to stretch him. Although disabled and vulnerable, our over-protecting him and not expecting him to tie his laces, tell the time, count money and develop personal skills necessary to survive in life, were compounding his vulnerability.

We asked ourselves, how much of Jack's disability was due to neglect and how much was inherent? Nature or lack of nurture? Joy helped us to understand that there was no simple answer. Sometimes you just have to get on with what is happening now and not worry about the future. She woke us up to the reality of 'if you accept Jack, you must also accept his disability and deal with it or send him back'.

Jack looks like any other child and then something happens to remind you he has a disability. One day I was waiting patiently at the school gate. It was the end of the term and all the children bounced out clutching various arts, crafts and awards, Amy with her beautiful portraits, George with the dance and performance trophy and Jack grasping a bag full of old carrier bags! He thought they might come in useful! He was happy with his collection of carrier bags and quite oblivious to all the other children's achievements. He embarrassed me at first and then I saw the funny side of it all. It didn't matter anyway. His success in life was always going be different from that of his peers.

Isn't that what disability means?

As time goes on I realise how shallow I was and probably still am. Ed had accepted Jack's limitations before Joe and I did. I now understand why social workers spend so much time during your assessment untangling your childhood. Like Joe's family, mine has a history of people with disabilities and difficulties. I have to admit Jack's disability set alarms bells ringing for me because I didn't want that burden again. I had wanted siblings I could relate to and feel equal to, but I didn't have them, and sadly we put Joe in the same position.

I think acceptance is a process many parents have to go through. Most do it gradually as they watch their child develop over the years – when they fail to achieve whatever they had hoped for, or make career choices perhaps not quite to the parents' liking – but the important thing is that they know their child is a decent and talented person in their own right. It's the same for us with Jack, only we had less time to get there.

Expectations are such a bother; they get in the way all the time. I needed reminding that my children were not born to me, they lived their early childhood in a different world from ours, they were born with different genetic blueprints than ours, so why should they be like us? Jack helped us all to get our adoptive family into perspective.

15

Empty again

RUTH

Joe's birth mother hadn't made contact through the letterbox managed by social services for five years now. Joe had mentioned it earlier in the year, but in such a casual way that I had assumed he wasn't that bothered. Joy put me right. He was bothered; anybody would be, especially a thirteen-year-old trying to work out how he fitted into the world. So we decided to try and trace his birth mother to re-instate the letterbox.

We talked to Joe and we agreed to contact WMPAS (West Midlands Post Adoption Service) to see if they could help. Up until then, Joe had been very private; he understood the need to be selective when talking about his past, and wasn't one of those children who blurted out gory details most people would rather not know.

One evening during half-term week, Joe and I visited his birth brothers. It was a particularly good day, but then he was especially horrible to Jack when we got home. This was deeply upsetting because he physically injured Jack, something he had not done before. Consequently Joe was sent off to his bedroom early; it wasn't so much for the injury he had inflicted as for the lack of concern about the pain he had caused Jack. He appeared to have no remorse and I wondered if he was really recovering from his early experiences after all. Did he still have a wall, or in his case, reams of cling film around him?

I couldn't sleep, and was up making coffee at about one in the morning when I heard Joe shuffling around in his bedroom. I knocked and went in. We sat on the bed chatting for ages. What emerged was a desperately sad boy. He sobbed as he told me how he wanted his brothers to live with us because I was so good with his younger brother and Dad would be so good for his older brother. We could be happy together. Even after nearly ten years he still hankered for them to be together, although his older brother's dysfunctional relationship with him meant they barely spoke, and his younger brother was unable to speak because of his disability. Joe's despair touched us all. Jack, unfortunately, took the brunt of it, with a smack around the head.

We talked honestly and openly together that night, and we cried together too, and somehow from that day Joe seemed a lighter and more together person. We agreed that tears were a better way to release sadness than walloping somebody over the head. He said some other children had said he was an empty person. This had made him feel deeply unhappy and confused.

It made me feel the same way, so at three o'clock in the morning I emailed Joy expressing my concerns. This is part of her reply:

> *This is positive, although I'm sorry Jack got hurt. Joe is playing out what happened to him as a young child and going through the process of bereavement about his family. This process is very much about loss of his brothers – even though that relationship has been negative in the past. He's blaming it on Jack but it's more about him having to share you than*

about Jack himself.

Maybe he can be helped to see why he is so destructive in his attempt to escape these painful feelings. Do not take anything he says as personal or as a rejection of you. Hear it as empty without his birth family and feeling full when with you. Then you can empathise with him.

As always, she made us see the positive side.

I suppose most parents must feel their children withdrawing from them as they start on their road towards independence but our time with our boys will have been short, and deep down there is the fear that their birth families still have the potential to hurt them. But equally they have the capacity to give them that feeling of connection we all need. So you worry a lot. Well, I do, anyway. And of course we don't want to lose Joe, but we know that he needs to feel good about himself, and that might mean sharing him or even losing him.

After several telephone calls and a few months of waiting, WMPAS found Joe's birth mother. Soon after, a letter with photos arrived. The relief that this one small letter gave him was magical. He asked many sensible questions, mostly about looks, health and life ambitions. All things any thirteen-year-old would want to know about his family. Joe wouldn't admit it has made a difference, but the rest of us could see it had. We got Joe back, and he was able to start enjoying his life again. Other pupils at school noticed that his attitude changed and his teachers commented on it in his end of year report.

For a short while I felt like a peripheral person in Joe's life. His birth mother could give him something I couldn't. I was no longer at the heart of his world and I didn't like it. Watching someone replace you, sideline you, is not pleasant. But in the end we knew it was best for him. He was happier and healthier knowing the answers to questions that most of us take for granted. It was becoming ever more important as he struggled with his identity and became more confident. Given the right emotional support, he would hopefully reach independence eventually.

Jack was different. His disability meant his capacity to attain basic life skills was limited. And no matter how many well-meaning social workers and teachers said 'but he gets on with people, that will get him through', I knew in my heart that was nonsense. Having worked for a local authority, training young people who couldn't find employment or education, I knew the ability to read, write and add up was essential for survival in the modern world. And yes, there were employment schemes for disabled people and sheltered housing, but they were generally for the severely disabled, not the Jacks of this world.

Ed and I had lots of conversations about how this might affect our retirement; did we want to be supporting an adult in our old age? It threw up many uncertainties for us that we hadn't confronted or planned for. And then it dawned on me why people adopt disabled children: disability strips away your vanity and puts your ego in its place. It wasn't Jack, it was me who had the problem. Loving Jack finally changed my reality, touched my heart and showed me the beauty of simply being a human being. Living isn't about the past or the future, it is about the here and now. Other people have children or siblings with far greater disabilities than Jack, and they manage by being compassionate and caring.

So, two years and seven months after he came to live with us, we went to court and adopted Jack. It was a lovely occasion and, as Ed said, we were all ready to move on. Dressed in all our finery we sat in the judge's private chambers, while he talked to the boys. He asked Jack to draw him a picture for his gallery: a gallery of pictures by all the children he had been lucky enough, he said, to declare adopted.

This hasn't meant that everything in the garden is rosy. Like in any family, our dynamics are always changing; every day we understand more about each other and from time to time an incident will remind us of how far we have come. Recently Joe was told off for some misdemeanour. I was getting somewhat overwrought, when he stood back, put his head on one side and, with a big grin, said, 'I think you're losing the plot here, Mum'. My ranting didn't trigger him into fight or flight mode; he was able to rationalise, step back, and best of all, make a joke out of it. I smiled, laughed and said 'Thanks!'

Joe has now taken to fashion in a big way, especially hairstyles and colour. One school holiday his hair changed from blonde to blue to green and back to blonde all in two weeks. He spent months growing it to his shoulders and then cut it very short. It was like he was trying to work out who he was. All very normal stuff, but what was different for him was his new-found confidence to share it with the outside world. He revelled in it, as well as in the attention it brought with it.

Soon after his adoption, I took Jack to visit my father in New Zealand. Originally, we had planned for all of us to go at Christmas but my father had been seriously ill and the pressure of having four of us to stay was too great. So Jack (whom he'd not met) and I went on our own.

ED

After Joe's thirteenth birthday, Ruth went to visit her father in New Zealand and Joe and I had three weeks alone together. It was surprisingly pleasant! I managed to get him to co-operate with the washing and cleaning, and any other request from me was met with a helpful 'yes'. He still moaned about my cooking, however. Joe says we got on because I let him do what he wanted. I think this is true, but what he cannot see is that I let him do what he wanted, to a certain extent, because he was helpful, pleasant and let me be in charge. Either way, this positive period has proved to him that we can get on together and, hopefully, when I next try to get him to do something with me, he will look back on that time and say 'yes'. Although I am not holding my breath!

RUTH

It was a low-key holiday, as my father couldn't have coped with lots of travelling or excitement. So, for the most part we stayed at home and did the occasional trip out to bird sanctuaries and cafés. Jack loved this, especially all the unusual birds, but he was always keen to return to my father's home.

Living next to my father were two brothers about Jack's age, with whom he played. They spent hours cycling around the traffic-free streets and roads, climbing trees and playing tag. The two brothers also had learning difficulties. Jack fitted in to their world of play. When their mother introduced herself she explained that she had a mild learning difficulty too. For Jack, it must have felt like a glimpse of his birth family, but with a mum and dad who coped. For me, it was an uncomfortable reminder of how tough he must find living with us.

Surprisingly, Joe accepted Jack and me going to New Zealand without him, although he made several requests for various luxury items to be brought back for him. Ed and Joe had the best three weeks of their entire ten years together. Did Joe feel less secure, and did that make him co-operate? Or was it less challenging emotionally for him because Jack and I weren't around? I don't know, but it was a surprise and gave us all some space. It has to be said, however, that Joe was especially difficult on our return, when we four were back together again.

For Ed and me, knowing that our boys are so much more needy than other children has been a gradual realisation. It has taken us a long time to see that they require so much more time, love, care and help to get over the hurt they have felt because their original families failed them. We watch them grow up, knowing that they don't resemble us in many ways at all, but we also know that without them life would be dull, even empty.

16

Walking again

ED

I have not found writing this book easy. The last time I did any creative writing was in the fifth form for Miss Smith some thirty-five years ago. I was in love with Miss Smith but I only just scraped an "O" level in English and that was where I left it.

The bit of this book I have most enjoyed writing was at the beginning, about the day's walk before we met Joy, so when I was stuck for an interesting way to end my half of the story, I realised it was September again, and my birthday, so why not have another day walking six years later and see what happens. I felt I could just do with a nice quiet day on my own. Ruth said great, go ahead, so I started to plan.

A couple of years ago we had a pleasant day in Birmingham and enjoyed walking along the canals. I got the maps out. We live close to a good rail link to Birmingham and luckily the canal follows the line down to Worcester. The plan was that Ruth would drop me off at the station after work. I would get the train up to Birmingham, have a curry, stay in a basic hotel, get up early, walk down the canal towards Bromsgrove and get the train to Worcester where Ruth would pick me up with the boys.

That night in bed Ruth said: 'You know what you should do, don't you? You should ask Joe to go with you. It would make a great chapter.'

I have to say I was not too keen. Joe rarely wanted to do anything I wanted to do at the best of times. If he did agree to come, I could see my quiet day going down the drain.

'He won't walk sixteen miles,' I said.

Ruth was convinced he would. 'All right,' I said, 'You sound him out.'

The next evening after work she said, 'He's keen'.

'He hasn't got any boots.'

'He can wear trainers, people run the marathon in trainers, you're only walking along a towpath!'

It looked as if we were going together. Joe said that he would have to be back for his Youth Group, and I promised to get him back in time.

On the day, I packed my backpack with fruit cake, and two packets of Cheddars, put on my boots and coat and stood at the door ready to leave. Joe was in a chaotic state, as usual creating a minor drama and threatening to pull out of the trip altogether. He said he had to go in his best clothes: his only decent jeans and top.

I said, 'Who do you think is going to see you on a Brum towpath?' He was adamant. I picked up his bag; it was heavy.

'What have you got in here?'

'I have to take my shampoo, conditioner and hair straighteners.'

Trying not to sound like the old bore he thinks I am, I said: 'Remember, if you take them, you will have to carry them all the way there and home again.'

'I am not going unless I can take them.'

We persuaded him to get in the car. Ruth and Jack took

us to the station and left us standing together on the platform. Ruth said later that we looked like a pair of lost souls, terrified of what the next twenty-four hours might bring. I was not really terrified but I did wonder what I would do if Joe refused to carry on after the first twenty minutes of walking. I consoled myself with the belief that he wanted this to work as much as I did.

The train was pretty full of mums and kids probably travelling home from a fairly boring half-term visit. They looked pretty fed-up but relaxed. Joe, on the other hand, looked like a startled rabbit caught in the headlights. Was it the thought of the big city, of travelling on a train or of being alone with me in unfamiliar territory? He borrowed my Ipod, plugged himself in, and in that raised voice people employ when listening to loud music through headphones, spent the whole journey moaning about my taste in music. I sat and looked out of the window – my favourite pastime on trains.

When we arrived at New Street station, I was determined to look like I knew what I was doing, or Joe would panic. He would also take great pleasure in telling all and sundry afterwards that I had got him lost straight off the train. I took a chance and started walking. I saw a street name; I was heading the right way. As we walked, we passed interesting, vaguely gothic looking Victorian buildings with beautiful arched windows and brick detail. I pointed them out to Joe and he said, 'They're very dirty.'

It is frustrating when Joe's attitude gets in the way. I would love to talk to him about things like architecture but most of the time he sees any interest as a sign of weakness. I know this is a teenage thing, but with Joe it has always been there. We carried on walking and in ten minutes we were at the hotel. So far so good, and we went up to the room.

'It's not very big,' said Joe, and settled down to check out the television. 'There are lots of horror films and it only costs ten pounds.'

'I have not come to the bright lights of the big city to spend the evening sitting in a hotel watching a film.'

We shared a bar of chocolate then went next door to the pub. I sat down with my pint. I thought, 'I have got to get him talking in sentences of more than five words otherwise it's going to be a very long evening.' I could not think of a subject he would want to talk about, so I asked him about his friends at school. Who fancies who, and was there any scandal? I was working on the theory that they all love *Eastenders*, so they all love to gossip. I was right. After his second coke he started to open up. We were really getting somewhere. He told me about the girls in his year. For the first time I felt he wanted to talk about his life outside the home. Maybe this trip wasn't going to be so bad after all.

The barman came over. 'I am sorry sir, our licence does not cover young people after eight. You will have to leave.'

I never have this problem out in the sticks. The banishment made Joe nervous again and he kept nagging to leave. I said I wanted to finish my drink.

We walked up through the jewellery quarter of Birmingham to a Chinese restaurant. Joe likes Chinese food, and I had found a good one on the internet the week before and marked it on the map. As we walked along, looking like I knew downtown Birmingham like the back of my hand, I steered the conversation round to how he felt, and was he happy? What could we do to make his life more enjoyable? When we sat down in the restaurant I suggested some things he could do to help himself. He listened and discussed everything rationally while he tucked into his chicken satay and special fried rice. He made the point that when we stopped his computer privileges for something he did, the ban went on for weeks, but for Jack it only lasted a matter of hours. I explained that Jack admits the problem and apologises quickly but he, Joe, escalates the situation and as a direct result the punishment becomes greater and longer. Joe seemed to accept and understand. It remains to be seen if his behaviour will change as a result of this revelation.

By the time the meal ended we were both very chatty and relaxed. I had had a couple of beers, which always makes me talk too much, and he was just happy. We walked back to the hotel discussing the various weird things to be seen in a city at night. I didn't know whether the evening would change anything, but at least we had some fun together. I went to bed feeling good. I lay in bed thinking that the next time he says to me, 'You don't understand, you never listen to me,' I can remind him that one evening we really talked, just the two of us.

I had planned to miss the continental breakfast and set off at eight o'clock, but Joe wanted a drink and cereal. So just before nine, Joe hoisted his pack, hair straighteners and all, and we walked out into a slightly foggy morning and set off down the canal at a good pace. Joe was quiet. The evening out was over and it was probably dawning on him that we were going to be walking for the next sixteen miles. I had planned to find a good greasy spoon about ten o'clock for a late breakfast. We made good time out of Birmingham, swapping tin-shedded industrial estates for the railway and the odd trendy block of apartments. A bit before ten we got to Aston University and I asked a couple of students if there was a café near by. They directed us through the campus and we had to walk against the tide of students heading in for the day. I pointed out to Joe that maybe one reason for working towards university was that there were so many attractive female students, but he was not impressed. Joe is bright but we always said we would not push him to go to university. We just want him to cope in the real world and I am not sure the stress of higher education would help him to do that. If he were keen to go without us nagging, we would be pleased. I didn't say any more.

We found the greasy spoon and tucked into a full English amongst the yellow jackets and copies of the *Daily Sport*. Trying to get back to the canal from the High Street we had to cross a cleared development site. We picked our way between the fly tipping. Joe looked uncomfortable.

'It's so dirty,' he said.

I thought, 'He is such a delicate flower out in the big bad world.'

We regained the security of the well-ordered canal and walked on steadily, burning off the fry up. About twelve o'clock, at the end of a tree shrouded cutting, the canal disappeared into the mouth of a tunnel and we were forced up out of the cutting into a high-rise housing estate. The path wasn't marked and we had to wander around in a suburban sprawl of back doubles and cul-de-sacs. Joe was becoming tetchy and nervous. I wondered if this place was bringing back memories of his early life on a rough estate. Living in the country, he rarely sees these kinds of places. After the housing estate we had to cross some rough ground and Joe's trainers became wet and he complained that his feet hurt. He was going downhill rapidly. I checked the map and luckily there was a pub marked just after the end of the tunnel. I encouraged him with talk of multiple cokes and a pub lunch. The route came down off the hill and we found the canal again. I towed Joe round the last bend, moaning and groaning, straight into the pub.

It was a bit of a "Steakhouse" but it was open and serving food. Neither of us was that hungry after the big breakfast. I had a bowl of soup. Joe wanted to skip the first two courses and went straight to the ice cream sundae. This didn't seem the best idea on a long walk, but I wasn't going to start a row over an ice cream, as his continued co-operation was already hanging by a thread. The coke idea was scrapped for a Red Bull. Usually I'd try to discourage him from drinking Red Bull, but as they say in the ads, "It gives you wings", and that was what he needed. I was sure he only had two, but he says he had three. Either way, he took off from the pub like a bat out of hell. He walked so fast I couldn't keep up with him. We tore across the Midlands for about an hour and I eventually caught up at the top of a hill above another tunnel. When I finally got my breath back we ate some fruitcake and he said, 'What time does the train go from Bromsgrove?' I said there was one at 3.15 and one at 4.15.

'I want to get the 3.15.'

'Why?'

'I want to go to Youth Group tonight.'

'You will never make the 3.15. If we catch the 4.15 it will give you enough time to shower and get there on time.'

'But I have to wash these clothes and dry them before I go.'

'Can't you wear something else?'

'I have nothing else to wear!'

Off he went at full speed to catch the early train. This was not what I had wanted. We needed to walk steadily and catch whichever train was convenient. Joe was turning the day into a race against time to fit in what he wanted to do. I had said I would try and get him to his Youth Group, but had not reckoned with laundering his clothes as well. Once he realised he was not going to make the earlier train, he started to slow down. You could almost see the effects of two Red Bulls and an ice cream sundae wearing off, as he got slower and slower and more and more miserable. About a mile from Bromsgrove he stopped altogether. I tried to explain that if we did not get going we would miss the 4.15 and he would certainly miss his Youth Group. He managed to summon enough energy to tell me that I would regret taking him on this walk and that he would never go walking with me ever again.

We left the canal and followed country lanes towards the station. Joe staggered on, intermittently removing his shoes and walking in his socks. I wanted to make that 4.15

train because if he did not get to his Youth Group I would have failed to deliver my side of the bargain and I would never hear the end of the story. I finally managed to drag him to the station and we only just caught the train. I phoned Ruth and told her we were on the train making for Worcester.

The train was packed and we had nowhere to sit. Joe was looking a bit of a mess, only to be expected after walking sixteen miles, but he was turning an alarming shade of white. We were only twenty minutes from Ruth, the car and salvation, when Joe announced that he was going to be sick. I had visions of projectile vomiting on a crowded commuter train. We got off and sat on a bench, and watched our train roll down the line and disappear from view. Joe was not only white, he was starting to shake. I wrapped him up in my fleece, found a café and bought him a hot chocolate. After a while he recovered.

'When is the next train?' he asked.

'In another hour.'

'What! I'll miss Youth Group! Then how long until we get there?'

'Twenty minutes.'

'This is all your fault!'

I tried to phone Ruth to tell her we had got off the train but the nice lady from Virgin informed me her phone had run out of credit. Despite my best intentions, the wheels were rapidly coming off, as the saying goes. All I could do was wait for the next train, hope Ruth would realise we had missed the first one and wait for the next. After an hour Joe looked better; we caught the next train and Ruth and Jack were there to meet us. Joe hobbled to the car, wrapped in my fleece, and left me to carry his knapsack. We drove home.

I had hoped when we got indoors Joe would go off the idea of Youth Group and settle down in front of the TV, but no such luck; he was up the stairs, showered, changed into his least unwearable clothes in ten minutes, and waiting by the car for me to drive him to his meeting. I think he wanted to announce he had just walked sixteen miles. I was determined to get him there because those were the terms we had agreed. I was exhausted both physically and mentally, but for the first time I felt we had accomplished something as a team. Up until then I had never been sure I could do it; or, worse still, that he would ever let it happen. That day proved it could happen and, best of all, I knew I could make it happen.

17

Our boys

RUTH

People used to talk about the adoption triangle consisting of the child, the birth parents and the adopters. After ten years of being an adoptive parent, I think it should be a diamond made up of child, adopted family, birth family and therapist. The diamond shape is more pleasing to look at and diamond stones radiate light, whereas a triangle is a mathematical inward looking shape. Diamonds are excellent abrasives and can be shaped by other diamonds – a fitting symbol of adoption.

Society recognises that the victims of airplane crashes, terrorist attacks and such like events need years of support, counselling or therapy, but take a child away from the two most important people in their lives, and it seems they have just got to get on with it. Even if children have the most hopeless or cruel parents, they will grieve if they lose them; the fact that they were negligent or abusive simply adds another layer of difficulty for the child to comprehend. For what it's worth, I believe there should be therapeutic intervention, direct work with the adopters and child, or at least ongoing expert therapeutic advice as part and parcel of *every* adoption plan.

Whatever the circumstances, when birth parents fail to form a positive and fulfilling bond with their children, as with both our boys, it leaves an enormous gap. Much of the time, our boys are like any other children but from time to time the emptiness returns, and they go through a spell of sadness. Joe said he felt like an Easter egg, all hollow inside. Jack said it felt like his heart had been torn in two. We see our boys live with that. Not daily and not always, but we know when either or both feel empty because it rubs off on us. Joe's sadness can swamp us and suck us in, whereas Jack's irritates more and adds stress to our lives. If I have learnt anything over the past ten years, it is the need for us to feel and acknowledge the boys' emotions. It is essential to share their trauma and grief to gain their trust. In a sense, if we ignore their feelings about their past, we are adding another layer of neglect.

Equally, I now realise the dangers of getting drawn into their trauma. There is a term to describe the transfer of one person's trauma to another: secondary traumatic stress disorder. When you connect, you feel their pain and even re-live it. Or sometimes it can feel like they are pushing you to mimic the actions of their birth parents. I have found myself wagging my finger at Jack and arguing with Joe until we were snarling like two wild cats; at one stage Ed and I both became as angry as our two boys – we reflected how they were feeling inside. So it is with caution that I say, 'try to feel what the child feels', but it worked for us.

Sixteen years ago when I was diagnosed with cancer, Ed and I, both only in our early thirties, talked endlessly about it – the big C. Quite understandably it dominated our lives, we didn't talk about it with other people much, but when alone we discussed it incessantly, every detail, every eventuality, the treatment, the future and the agonising uncertainty. Until one day, two years after the original diagnosis, Ed quietly said to me, 'I don't want to talk about cancer anymore; if we do, it will take over our lives forever, and in a sense it will win the battle'. I felt deeply hurt, but accepted what he said.

So it occurred to me that perhaps this is how our boys feel. Cancer was a traumatic event in our lives. The neglect and abuse they have suffered was traumatic too. I was an adult, so I can recall the story of my disease with clarity, and I have the vocabulary to express myself, and to make sense of it all. But our boys were too young to rationalise and make sense of their stories because they, especially Joe at three years of age, lacked the language and life experience. So they have been left with mixed, confused and overwhelming emotions.

Even now I can recall the actual moment the consultant told me I had cancer, his every word and gesture are imprinted on my brain forever. I shall never forget his hands. They were small and child-like and made his white coat look too big for him. He rubbed them together as he answered my question. What did malignant mean? I can't believe I didn't know.

So our boys who each lived for three years in chaos, and sometimes with violence, are brave little soldiers carrying huge bags of kit, filled with trauma, on their backs. Hopefully Joy has helped us to lighten their load and given them the tools to understand their early lives and how they have been affected. There was an incident one Saturday morning that showed the difference in the boys' remaining difficulties. I went into the kitchen to find a piece of china, of sentimental value, broken. It had belonged to my mother. I was livid. The boys were not moved in the slightest. I went to Ed's office and cried. Jack hovered by the door becoming increasingly upset that I was upset. Joe, now thirteen, was trying to get Jack to make peace with me. It was like he couldn't do it, couldn't admit he cared.

Eventually Jack's scratching around at the door roused me to open it. Jack presented me with a card he had rustled up. He had drawn a bird on the front and it said 'sorry' inside. Both boys had signed it. I accepted Jack's apology and we hugged. Joe on the other hand wasn't prepared to do the face-to-face 'I'm sorry' bit. He did eventually say sorry but even now he still needs guidance with intimacy, something that comes more naturally to Jack. I know the boys have different personalities, but it is more fundamental than that. Joe still struggles to empathise, and make sense of others' feelings and behaviour.

It has taken time for our boys to attach to each other. I am not suggesting that they have a healthy strong relationship, but they are certainly not indifferent to each other. Starting from a month-long honeymoon, which quickly sank into mutual loathing, they somehow grew to respect each other; loyalty developed and a bond, albeit shaky, was created. Now we are in the trivial bickering and the occasional thumping each other phase. But the other night Joe read two chapters of *The Hobbit* to Jack. A lot can happen – it doesn't just happen overnight; it is a process, full of ups and downs and merry go-rounds.

The key to unlocking the boys' trauma was Joy's music and art. Without her we would never have had the confidence to challenge Joe's and Jack's perceptions of the world. In their own ways they both created a bubble around themselves, which is what we all do if we are threatened. But their bubbles excluded intimacy and close relationships. Joy's music, and to some extent art, helped us to penetrate their bubbles. We went to her as a family out of rhythm and out of tune, each making our own sound but not keeping time or making music together. If we played instruments together today it wouldn't be perfect, but it would be more co-operative, more fun, more open and trusting. We would enjoy it.

As much as I would love to say that therapists like Joy perform miracles and cure your child, I can't. She hasn't "cured" either of our boys, but she did make a difference.

Looking back, I'm not sure we would have survived as a family without her, and I am quite sure about the positive impact therapy had on both boys, but especially on Joe, because he needed something powerful and fundamental to shift his perception of the world adults create.

There has been a gradual, and I mean gradual because it is still very much "work in progress", improvement in how Joe communicates. He looks people in the eye and he tries to connect instead of retreating into his detached, cut-off world. He no longer wants to be hollow. He wants some of the good feelings we all get when we click with fellow human beings.

Joe is lucky because he is good looking and has a rather quirky sense of humour and is reasonably bright. As he makes his way through the turmoil of the teenage years, we are watching him turn into a person who wants to live a full life. He recently said to me, 'I don't want to be on the edge any more'. Joy helped him join the human race.

There are still issues for Joe. He still has difficulty asking for help, often puts up barriers to protect himself against possible rejection, can appear to have an attitude, lacks empathy and can be entirely wrapped up in himself. Some of this is normal adolescence and some has roots further back. We can help him grow, but in the end we can't change his past and the emotional disability it has left him. He is recovering but it is a life-long task. With Joy's help, we have merely equipped him better for his journey.

Jack is very different indeed. He worked with Kate, the art therapist, as much as he worked with Joy. Kate skilfully helped Jack to see himself as a whole person, rather than Jack the clown, whose only role in life was messing around, making others laugh and hiding behind his cute smile. They worked together on building up a beautiful picture of his life story, which helped him get the facts straight but never touched, moved or engaged him emotionally. We will soon be taking a trip back to see Joy.

Jack's schoolwork has improved slightly during his three years with us. He can concentrate better and does read a bit, but should be achieving more. No one had been able to pinpoint why he wasn't learning until a few weeks ago, when he told me how his birth father physically threatened him when he was unable to remember his letters and numbers. He is afraid that a mistake will put his life in danger. Every time he tries to read he has to cope with all the feelings his birth father aroused in him. So we are going back to see Joy in the hope that she can release him from his terror and, who knows, that may help his learning difficulties.

For me, every aspect of therapy has been worth it because of all the support and practical advice we have had. Joy was able to explain behaviour that seemed outrageous and beyond our understanding. Initially we participated in the boys' therapy sessions, but more lately Ed and I have attended workshops organised by Joy and her team. These have proved invaluable because so much has been discovered about trauma and how it affects a child's development generally, and more specifically, the infant brain; how the effects of emotional neglect and abuse disable a child from using this most vital part of their body. It relegates parts of their brain to a wheelchair, disables them intellectually as with Jack, or emotionally, as with Joe.

There is a lot of misunderstanding around adoption, and pretending that tender loving care is enough to compensate for early trauma only adds to it. Over the years we have found most people treat adoption as they used to treat cancer patients. You knew they were ill but didn't think you should talk about it or acknowledge it. People who know the children are adopted don't feel comfortable talking about it because they are afraid to offend or intrude. They don't mean to, but they are adding to the adoption myth. And that myth goes back a long way to the fairy tales and children's stories that involve adoption. In all these stories there are elements of mystery and evil, which are untangled and come good in the end. If mystery and evil are not untangled, then the likelihood of good triumphing over evil is greatly reduced. If an adopted child is to grow into a fulfilled adult, then adopters, unlike other parents, have the job of unravelling the mystery. In our case, therapy helped us to do that.

Our boys are exceptional for us, because they are ours. But they are not exceptional; they are typical of children who have been removed from their birth families by the state to protect them from neglect and abuse – children who have been adopted when they are past infancy.

Sometimes I wonder, in fifty years' time, will social historians look back at this phase of adoption in the same way as we now regard sending children off to Australia in the middle nineteen hundreds? Will we be thought of as well meaning, misguided fools? Will there be stories in the media showing how over-zealous social workers removed children from their families of origin? If I'm confused and uncertain, what about the children? What will they think of it all?

After living here for over thirty years I still can't quite feel English. I love the landscapes, the laughter, the questioning, the small terraced houses that are castles inside, the endless possibilities, roads and lanes everywhere, *Newsnight* and *Question Time*, hedgerows and trees, but I am not English, never will be nor want to be. No, to be English I would have to give up part of myself and I can't do that. I can't give up the New Zealand part of me because that's where my roots are, where I came from. And although I know I will never live there again, I still have a fantasy of returning to a place with bold blue skies, fruit and vegetables with flavours, peace and quiet, simplicity and dense, mysterious bush land. My childhood home, like most people's, wasn't perfect but it is still the place in the world with special meaning for me, even after over thirty years of exile. Is that how it feels for a child taken away from their origins? Joe was only three when he was removed, but the first three years are the vital years, the years when the brain develops and impressions are formed subconsciously but most powerfully.

The magnetic pull towards your origins draws you back, no matter what the memories, with such force that the past can dominate your life. Why should our adopted children give up their identities? Why should it be less important for them because their parents have made mistakes, or broken the law? Who knows, in fifty years' time we may understand better why people abuse or neglect their children, and we may then be able to treat the cause rather than the symptoms. Anything is possible. By the time our children are adults with families of their own, some of the reasons why they were separated from their birth families, and adopted, may no longer be valid.

Whatever the future holds, I need to hold on to some of my New Zealand past and I hope our boys can hold on to some of their past. I hope they will, but I must admit to worrying that they might one day choose to go back rather than forward with us. I hope they can eventually do both.

I think the therapy Joy and her team offered us will help our boys to feel better about themselves and their families – birth and adoptive. It changed us forever; it gave us more insight into who we are and how we form relationships. It taught us how vital it is for parents to talk to their adopted children about the past, no matter how painful it is, and it enriched our communication as a couple: after eleven years together, sitting in a restaurant, Ed and I confided in each other about events that took place in our childhoods. It took us that long to share fears from when we were only eight and ten years old.

Our journey goes on, and it is sometimes very hard. There have been some bleak moments, thoughts and feelings, and revulsion about how cruel people can be. At times our family has felt fragile to the point we thought it might implode, with all four of us collapsing into a heap and the children being carted off into care. Part of our journey has been to recognise that we can all only do as much as we are capable of and that some things are beyond our control.

Sometimes I imagine us making music again. We gingerly choose our instruments, while Joy encourages us by playing a soothing melody on her upright piano. Joe rather reluctantly takes up his drumsticks, Ed, keen as ever, immediately gets going on a drum, and Jack and I tinker on the tambourine and a shaker. Joy's playing gets softer as Ed and Joe's drums get louder and faster. They beat the drums with all their energy, in time, and together while Jack and I blend in our more delicate sounds. We are all in tune as the piano fades into the background.

WITHDRAWN